Ready, Set, Potty!

of related interest

Liam Goes Poo in the Toilet
A Story about Trouble with Toilet Training
Jane Whelen Banks
ISBN 978 1 84310 900 6

Constipation, Withholding and Your Child
A Family Guide to Soiling and Wetting
Anthony Cohn
ISBN 978 1 84310 491 9

Caring for Myself
A Social Skills Storybook
Christy Gast and Jane Krug
Photographs by Kotoe Laackman
ISBN 978 1 84310 872 6 hardback
ISBN 978 1 84310 887 0 paperback

Joey Goes to the Dentist
Candace Vittorini and Sara Boyer-Quick
ISBN 978 1 84310 854 2

Ready, Set, Potty!

Toilet Training for Children with Autism and Other Developmental Disorders

Brenda Batts

Jessica Kingsley Publishers
London and Philadelphia

Illustrations in Figures 8.1 and 8.4 reproduced with kind
permission from The Picture Communication Symbols © 1981–
2009 by Mayer-Johnson LLC. All Rights Reserved Worldwide.
Boardmaker™ is a trademark of Mayer-Johnson LLC.

First published in 2010
by Jessica Kingsley Publishers
73 Collier Street
London N1 9BE, UK
and
400 Market Street, Suite 400
Philadelphia, PA 19106, USA

www.jkp.com

Copyright © Brenda Batts 2010

Library of Congress Cataloging in Publication Data
A CIP catalog record for this book is available from the Library of Congress

British Library Cataloguing in Publication Data
A CIP catalogue record for this book is available from the British Library

ISBN 978 1 84905 833 9

Printed and bound in the United States by
Thomson-Shore, 7300 Joy Road, Dexter, MI 48130

ACKNOWLEDGMENTS

As a parent of a child with autism and a professional serving children with special needs, I understand the challenges involved in teaching our children skills to ensure that they can be all that they are designed to be, skills critical to guide them on the road to independence. This book is dedicated to the hundreds of thousands of parents and teachers who have been successful in implementing the potty training skills discussed in this book. This book could never have been written without the inspiration that God has given me, or without the support of friends and family who have encouraged me.

I wrote this book in order to help the thousands of parents and teachers, who are in search of practical solutions to help address the many potty training challenges that their children with special needs encounter. This book is dedicated to my sons Alex and JR, who have taught me that there is no limit to living, loving, and learning, and to my loving husband Douglas, who has been a pillar of support and encouragement throughout the years. I wish to offer a very special thanks to the countless numbers of children with special needs whom I have worked with over the past 25 years, from whom I have learned great lessons of patience, love, and hope. Finally, I give thanks to the wonderful parents and teachers of those children with special needs who have shared their trials and triumphs with me. Thank you for sharing your precious angels with me.

With gratitude,
Brenda M. Batts, M. Ed

CONTENTS

CHAPTER 1

INTRODUCTION

The road to independence

"I dread potty training my daughter, I know that it will be very difficult."

Potty training is one of the most significant milestones for children, whether they have developmental disorders or not. For years, the issue of potty training has been a difficult one for parents and teachers of children with special needs. We as parents and teachers think of potty training as our responsibility: a responsibility that we feel entails our full involvement, without taking into consideration that the responsibility for potty training lies on the person being potty trained.

Potty training a child with autism or other developmental disorders or special needs is often difficult, because we view the potty training process as a stressful situation. The stress related to potty training issues is due to the absence of skills and knowledge that parents and teachers of children with special needs might have: knowledge and skills necessary to implement a potty training program that requires full understanding of the process, and knowledge of the skills necessary to achieve success. For children with autism and other developmental disorders, the stress in potty training originates from being introduced to a new concept, and their failure to acquire the necessary skills to understand the expectations involved in the process, coupled with their failure to generalize that concept, and be able to use their newfound learning across different environments. There are many potty training programs available for parents and teachers of children with developmental disorders, but they often lack specificity, and a clear map to help children achieve success. Parents and teachers may also see the potty training process as a huge task to undertake when in fact, the process of potty training children with developmental disorders is one of the easiest skills to teach, if we implement a program that has as its core principle the critical components of a successful program: order, predictability, and routine.

When parents and teachers attempt to potty train their child with developmental disorders, they often do so without taking into consideration that potty training is a process and not an event. Parents and teachers often decide to potty train their children without a specific plan, or without taking into consideration their own expectations, or their children's expectations. Since potty training is a process and not an event, a well-structured program must be designed, a program that involves writing a specific goal, which becomes the road map to implementing a successful program. This goal involves the expected outcome, and specific steps or objectives that break down the process, in order to facilitate the outcome.

Ready, Set, Potty! is a system that facilitates the potty training process for children, as well as for their parents and teachers. This program has been used with hundreds of thousands of children with special needs, and neuro-typical children all around the world with a high degree of success. Its success lies in its highly structured approach, and in its method of implementing a program that is clear, concise, and relevant for both parents and children with special needs. Ready, Set, Potty! has been successful in potty training children with varying degrees, or levels, of disability. This is a unique program that yields success anywhere between three and five days, depending on the child. Is this program a magic wand? No, what Ready, Set, Potty! is, is a method of viewing the child as a child first, and then a child with a disability. This approach to potty training provides parents, and teachers, with the necessary tools to facilitate the process for their children, and it offers parents and teachers an innovative and practical approach to tackle an otherwise difficult milestone for their children.

In the subsequent chapters, parents and teachers will explore the concept of an Individualized Teaching technique. This concept will help parents and teachers address the three key components involved in Ready, Set, Potty! and its effect on helping children with developmental disorders acquire the skills needed to successfully potty train. Parents will also learn to develop an individualized goal and objectives in order to design an individualized potty training plan. Issues of the difficulty in potty training children with developmental disorders will be addressed to help parents and teachers understand why the process is viewed as a difficult task to be accomplished. An effective potty training program explores the different areas that parents and teachers need to consider when helping their children to potty train; this discussion will lead to the actual steps involved. Another area that will be discussed in subsequent chapters involves the issue of picking a target day to begin the process, and a discussion of motivators versus rewards.

We will delve into the area of selecting a theme for our program, and discuss the importance of using visual supports to facilitate potty training. Developing individualized potty stories to address skills training will be discussed, and our potty training adventure will conclude with a wrap-up of the Ready, Set, Potty! program, along with common questions parents and teachers often ask when attempting to potty train children with special needs. Parents and teachers will also be given tips and samples after every chapter to help them visualize, and individualize, their own potty training program. So if you are ready to embark on the most amazing journey, let's get Ready, Set, Potty!

Before you begin

- Write down three reasons why you have experienced anxiety over potty training your child in the past.

- Isolate two reasons why you think potty training your child has not been successful in the past.

- Write down two obstacles that you think you might have to overcome to potty train your child.

- Write down three strategies that you can use to overcome potty training challenges.

- Write down five benefits for you, not for your child, in achieving potty training success.

A note on vocabulary

Throughout this book I have used a variety of words to refer to the bathroom/toilet/potty and what your child needs to learn to do there. When talking to your child choose simple words that you are happy to use as a family, such as "potty," "pee pee," and "poo poo," and use them consistently. Readers outside the USA should note that I use the word "potty" in the North American sense to refer to a toilet as well as to a child's potty.

CHAPTER

INDIVIDUALIZED TEACHING

What is Individualized Teaching?

> "I have been trying to potty train my son for well over a year. I have used several potty training programs and nothing seems to work; maybe he is not ready."

The readiness of a child's ability to successfully potty train is not, and should not be, dictated by the presence of a disability. Rather, a child's readiness to acquire the needed skill in order to successfully potty train is facilitated by the manner in which we, as parents and teachers, present the information to them. The presentation of the skills needed to potty train a child with special needs is facilitated by the use of an Individualized Teaching approach: an approach that offers the child clarity in instruction, while at the same time strengthening the child's information processing skills to successfully internalize, and subsequently perform, those skills with accuracy and consistency across different environments. What is an Individualized Teaching approach, and how does this approach facilitate the acquisition of potty training skills for children with developmental disorders? Furthermore, why should this technique be a part of a potty training program?

The beauty of Individualized Teaching

Let us explore the issue of Individualized Teaching. Individualized Teaching is an approach that views the child as a child first, and then a child with a disability. This technique takes into consideration a child's individual learning modes, and his or her unique way of processing and internalizing information. Individualized Teaching works on the premise that every child with special needs can learn when given the proper tools to do so. This approach addresses the notion that children do come with instructions; we, as parents and teachers, just have to learn to read those instructions properly. More than an approach, Individualized Teaching is a unique method of intervention that offers children with developmental disorders opportunities to learn, to grow, and to develop using a method that has as its main components order, predictability, and routine. A well-structured program to address potty training issues teaches the child the skills necessary to potty train, and at the same time educates parents and teachers alike on how to develop the type of program that will ensure success. In essence, a good potty training program is a program that trains the child, the parents, and anyone else involved in the process.

It is crucial for a successful program to take into account a child's individual learning mode. Accounting for our children's individual learning modes helps parents and educators design well-thought-out plans, and strategies to help our children become successful across different environments no matter how difficult the task might seem. This is particularly true for designing a successful training program. Children with developmental disorders encounter a variety of issues that can get in the way of them acquiring skills with ease. One of the issues revolves around addressing our children's challenges in processing the world around them; this is *the* main difficulty involved in potty training children with developmental disorders. Our children's difficulty with information processing can affect areas such as receptive/expressive communication, self-help skills, independence skills, and behavior in general.

Individualized Teaching alleviates most of the challenges affecting our children's information processing; this is particularly true for children with significant communication disorders. When parents and teachers use proactive skills to ensure that our children internalize new concepts, children are set up for success in regard to potty training, or any other skill we attempt to teach them. Since the Individualized Teaching approach takes into consideration our children's individual learning modes, we need to consider the different sensory issues that can affect learning of new skills for our children. Issues such as visual over/under-stimulation, vestibular, tactile, smell/taste, and proprioceptive issues, as well as our children's likes and dislikes, are areas that can limit our children's acquisition of new skills. What are the sensory issues that negatively or positively affect your child's learning? This is an important question to answer, in order to design a successful potty training program.

It is worth taking a brief visit into the area of sensory issues, in order to understand the difficulty our children experience when confronted by new learning, such as in the case of potty training. Sensory issues relate to the manner in which we integrate and process incoming information, and when the integration of incoming information is not received in a clear manner, a person may experience an inability to pull together and understand, or process information from the environment in an appropriate manner. Our senses give us information about the world around us; this information, when clear, helps us link to the world outside us, and create connections that facilitate the acquisition of new skills. In my years of working with children with special needs, I have found that children revert to repetitive behaviors when confronted with information that is unclear to them, or information with which they have no prior experience. In this instance, a child is taking a small break from the demands placed upon him or her, and taking refuge in a place or situation that offers him or her comfort. Some examples of sensory issues are:

1. Visual sensory stimulation

    - fixation with certain objects such as a ball, flickering his or her fingers, rewinding movies

    - avoids certain clothes or colors

    - avoids certain public places such as restaurants/ supermarkets

    - prefers to be in dark places

    - trouble going up or down stairs

    - avoids certain types of lights

    - stares intently at objects

    - avoids eye contact.

2. Vestibular movements

    - spinning self or objects, rocking back and forth, excessive jumping

    - excessive running, and throwing objects

    - significant temper tantrums

    - becomes distressed when feet don't touch the ground

    - seeks all kinds of movement

    - no safety awareness.

3. Tactile

    - fascination with certain objects or textures

    - sensitive towards certain textures/fabrics including clothes tags

- need for excessive pressure, high tolerance for pain, and takes exception to being touched in certain places
- changes in behavior because of temperatures
- avoids getting hands messy.

4. Smell and taste

- gets upset by certain odors
- smells non-food items routinely
- certain odors stimulate calm, or sends him or her into sensory overload
- seeks out certain smells/foods
- limited food choices
- avoidance of certain foods or smells.

5. Proprioceptive issues

- has the need to pull, or be pulled by someone
- constant kicking for no apparent reason
- seeks out all kinds of movement activities
- continually hangs on other people, furniture, and objects
- may have weak muscle tone, and/or fine/gross motor skills
- walks on toes.

As you can see, sensory integration challenges can significantly impair our children's ability to make sense of the world around them. Our children's sensory issues lead to significant behavior issues that interfere with their ability to process the information, and the resulting behaviors can get in the way of our children acquiring potty training success. Let's take a look at some of these behaviors:

- persistent inappropriate behaviors
- difficulties with motor control
- persistent oppositional behaviors
- fine/gross motor difficulties
- frequent irritability or moodiness
- oral motor difficulties that impact speech
- hypersensitivity to touch, sights, food intake, sounds, smells, or taste
- visual spatial deficits
- poor attention span
- clumsiness
- organizational deficits
- language deficits
- attention deficits
- temper tantrums
- sleep problems
- stress caused by over-stimulation
- transition difficulties
- throws self on floor
- screaming for no apparent reason
- takes off running in public places
- hits, kicks, bites
- argues all the time
- disorganized
- not independent in self-help skills
- temper tantrums
- unable to finish work/task

- inappropriate language/echolalia
- unmotivated
- destructive behavior
- covers ears/face
- hand flapping
- poor social skills.

Looking at the many sensory issues that our children are affected with, and the behaviors that accompany these issues, helps us understand why children with developmental disorders have difficulty in achieving potty training success. The recognition of these issues helps us, as parents and teachers, to design a potty training program that addresses these challenges in a proactive manner, keeping in mind that our children are more like us than they are different.

We as parents and teachers need to recognize that potty training issues are not unique to children with special needs. The issue of potty training is difficult for any parent. Do you remember when you were potty trained? Probably not, and if you do, you probably do not want to discuss the age at which you potty trained! Potty training is probably the most anxiety-ridden skill we ever had to learn as children, hence the reason why the process has been erased from our computer memory. In my personal experience as a mother of a child with moderate autism, I too encountered significant challenges when Alex was two years old and not potty trained. I used to joke with people that Alex would hand me his diapers on his way to the altar, since he seemed to be comfortable when wet. The biggest challenge for me was that Alex was non-verbal, and not able to voice his wants and needs; this led to severe behavior issues, and significant impairment in his ability to internalize new concepts. The problem did not lie with Alex's perceived inability to understand the potty training concept. Rather, the challenge lay with me, and my own deficit in recognizing that, in order for Alex to understand the expectations in regard to potty training, it was imperative to take into consideration his needs and wants, his mode of learning, and his individual differences in perceiving the world around him. Once I understood Alex's challenges, and my own limitations, I developed and implemented Ready, Set, Potty! and the use of the Individualized Teaching approach, and Alex was able to potty train in three days with no frustration on his part or mine. In fact, potty training became fun for both my son and me!

Tips for parents and teachers

- Think about three benefits of individualizing skills. Individualizing skills means to take into consideration a child's unique learning mode, likes, dislikes, and sensory issues, in order to develop and implement a program that is relevant and appealing to the child.

- Write down three strategies that would help you in individualizing a potty training program.

- Isolate three ways to individualize your child's potty training program.

- Answer the question as to how both you and your child would benefit in using an Individualized Teaching approach.

- Answer the question as to what has been some of the most difficult potty training issues in your past attempts.

CHAPTER

COMPONENTS OF A WELL-STRUCTURED PROGRAM

Order, predictability, and routine

In order to implement the Individualized Teaching approach in regard to potty training, we must understand the three critical components to the successful implementation of this method. Earlier we discussed that order, predictability, and routine were the backbone of the Individualized Teaching approach. Any program that seeks to change or modify any type of behavior requires a thorough understanding of the manner in which one seeks to accomplish that goal in order to ensure success.

The first component of the Individualized Teaching approach involves order. Order relates to the manner and sequence in which a potty training program is presented to the child. The issue of order provides children with clarity in instruction. Order facilitates our children's ability to learn new concepts, and to acquire the skills necessary to successfully potty train. Order helps children focus on specific and relevant information, thereby increasing their independence in the area of potty training, while helping them develop self-esteem due to them experiencing success. To be able to understand the importance of the concept of order, it is imperative to understand that our children are more like us than they are different. Think of a scenario where you can predict that you will have quite a few phone messages to return tomorrow when you go back to work. Imagine that in the morning, you got to work and discovered that your messages have no name, only a phone number, leaving you with no idea of whom you are supposed to be calling, or who called you first. Furthermore, your messages do not even state a reason for the call! In this scenario, your order has been broken, and you call the person who took your messages in the hope that he or she could remember that information. Your order has been tampered with, leaving you with no sense of how or what to do next. At that time, you know you have to re-organize, but how? Having only a phone number to return your calls leaves you with little information and you feel temporarily lost, until your problem solving skills take over the unpredictable situation.

Now go back to children with special needs, and the impact that a lack of order can have in their daily activities. What can the lack of order in regard to potty training do to our children's ability to internalize the needed skills? Without order in their activities, our children with special needs have no other option but to respond to the lack of clarity in instruction. The lack of order forces our children to resort to the familiarity of what they know, and more often then not, leads them to develop the type of problem solving skills that interfere with their ability to learn, execute, internalize, and generalize the expected skills. As I have said, our children are more like us than they are different. We all have an innate need to have order in our daily lives. Order helps us to perform the steps necessary to successfully complete a task; it offers us information as to what task is expected of us, how we are expected to perform it, and how much work is involved in performing a given task. The information that the concept of order provides us with helps us navigate through the steps that lead us to complete a given task. Without the information that order provides, our performance would skip some steps critical to the successful outcome of the task. Implementing visual order into a potty training system, using a sequence of images, helps children with special needs not only to visualize, but also to perform the steps needed to potty train.

Predictability is the second component of the Individualized Teaching approach. In the area of predictability, we aim to reinforce the child's expectations in regard to potty training using individualized, visual stories carefully sequencing the potty training expectations. Predictability helps to increase our children's understanding of expectations and appropriate behavior at home, at school, and in social situations. The ability to predict what will happen next helps our children visualize expectations, and once our children can visualize those expectations, predictability acts as a problem solving monitoring system that helps our children to internalize the sequence/steps in which a skill should be performed. The need to have predictability in what we are expected to do is not unique to children with special needs. Predictability is a human necessity that, when present in our lives, helps us to visualize the events of our day, thereby lowering our anxiety about what will happen, and how we are expected to perform a certain skill.

Imagine taking the same route to work every morning, something very familiar to you. This morning, road construction called for you to take another route, only to realize that you have to take yet another route due to more construction. Now you are lost, and your satellite navigation system is not picking up that unfamiliar country road. You know you are expected to show up to an early meeting but you are not sure what it is about, and you are running late. If you are anything like me, and like most of us, you stop to ask for directions, but this morning, it seems like everyone has conspired against you, because you keep getting the wrong directions. Most likely, after a while of being lost, you begin to feel anxious, then you feel angry, and pretty soon you lose the focus of your primary goal: to find your way back to that familiar road that will ultimately lead you to your place of work. With all these emotions, an onlooker would deduct that you are having some behavior issues, all because you are so angry, and your lack of focus has kept you from reading the signs that could help you get back on track to accomplish your goal. The lack of predictability in a poorly designed potty training program yields the same result as our example; it provides our children with the same feeling of being lost. The lack of predictability leaves our children with no reliable information to succeed in what we are asking them to accomplish. In the same line of thinking, when our children are presented with predictability, it helps them to listen to their bodies, and helps them respond to a need, a want, and a must. Our children with developmental disorders are more like us than they are different, and the issue of predictability confirms this reality.

The final, but no less important, component of the Individualized Teaching approach involves routine. Routine in regard to potty training helps children focus on specific and relevant information. Routine clarifies expectations, reduces behavior problems, and increases independence. Routine yields consistency and consistency provides the basis for teaching children with developmental disorders to acquire skills in any area. The consistency acquired through routine helps children retain newly acquired skills, while helping them strengthen and perfect the skills that lead to independence in potty training. A lack of consistency in regard to successfully potty training a child with special needs does not only pertain to the child themselves, but also to the person or persons in charge of potty training. Anything in life requires us to be consistent in our approach, in order to achieve success.

Consistency also relates to our children internalizing a routine about the skills involved in potty training. It tells our children, "This is what I need to do all the time, under all circumstances." Consistency also helps parents and teachers to train themselves to expect success. A lack of consistency in your past attempts to potty train your child should not be viewed as the only reason why your child has not successfully potty trained; this cannot be further from the truth. Although routine and consistency are critical in the potty training process, it is not the lack thereof that has kept you and your child from achieving success. Think of potty training as a chain. Every chain becomes a chain because of its individual links; links are important because without them, a chain is not a chain. When a chain is broken, it is probably because one of the links has disconnected, or because one of the links has broken. A broken link disconnects the chain from the rest of the links, and the information needed to continue to be a complete chain is not present; that chain ceases to be a chain. The potty training process is much like a chain. In your goal to potty train your child, you must look at the potty training chain and study it carefully to define which link has disconnected, and how to bring the chain together again, so that the links can begin to communicate with each other, and form a successful chain. This brings us back to the issue at hand: helping our children with developmental disorders to successfully potty train. The issue of order, predictability, and routine is critical to your goal, and when a potty training program targets these critical components, the only possible outcome is to succeed! The Individualized Teaching approach, through these main components, order, predictability, and routine, answers the questions: when, why, and for how long? These are questions that parents and educators should ask themselves before beginning a potty training program.

CHAPTER **4**

CRITICAL QUESTIONS

When, why, and for how long?

"Another try, what if it doesn't work?"

When, why, and for how long? These questions seem to resonate in our minds when we think of potty training our child with a developmental disorder. In order to answer these questions, we must consider specific issues involved in the potty training process. Several factors are involved in helping our children to potty train, and simply explaining these factors to our children will not facilitate the training process, in fact it will only bring more anxiety to a process that can be fun for both parents and children. Ready, Set, Potty! is a system that has been instrumental in helping many children with special needs potty train, because of its highly individualized and structured components. An individualized and structured approach calls for thorough understanding of the system we are about to implement, and a clear approach that can only be achieved when we clearly define the when, why, and for how long questions of our program.

The question of when you should start implementing a potty training program is an important one. This is a question that many parents of children with developmental disorders often ask, and teachers are baffled by this question as well. Many people think that in order for a child with a developmental disorder to potty train successfully, he or she must be able to verbally communicate, or show the clear signs of readiness that most neuro-typical children often display. This cannot be further from the truth. Children with developmental disorders *do* communicate. Maybe not in the same manner in which most neuro-typical children communicate, but our children with developmental disorders are masters at letting us know what they want, how they want it, and when they want it. The issue of potty training your child should not be based on chronological or developmental age either, because the majority of children with developmental disorders operate below their chronological age, and their developmental delays should not be impediments to learning. Rather, these developmental delays are to be approached from the point of view that our children are capable of learning, if we present them with information that is clear and concise. Take for example a child who is non-verbal. Think back to the many instances when you hid that cookie jar in the back of your pantry, when you thought your child was not watching you, and suddenly when she wanted a cookie, she pointed or pushed you towards the pantry. Likewise, think about the many times when your child actually climbed up to get something that he wanted. Your child was communicating to you what he wanted, and when he wanted it. In this example, your child has communicated his or her needs and wants behaviorally. It is right then that you realized that your child's communication and problem solving skills were beyond what you thought they were.

When I embarked on potty training my son, I noticed that he knew exactly what items he wanted, and not only that, he actually found a way to get them from me through his own actions. It was then that I realized that if my son could process all the information to get something that was of high importance to him, he could likewise point to the bathroom to let me know that he wanted to go to the toilet. My challenge was to make the potty training skill of high importance to him as well, by pairing it up with a high interest item for him.

When should you start potty training your child? There are hosts of behaviors to look for before you begin potty training. Looking at these behaviors will help you identify the time when you should begin your potty training program. Ready, Set, Potty! is a system that has been used worldwide to potty train children and adults with disabilities ranging from mild, to moderate, to severe, so your child's particular level of disability does not, and should not, prevent him or her from successfully potty training. After you can understand this concept, it is safe to move to answering the when, why, and for how long questions.

When should you potty train your child?

You should potty train your child when:

- he or she can communicate his or her needs and wants behaviorally, and/or verbally
- your child has preference in activities, foods, and/or toys
- your child asks for juice by pointing, verbally asking, or by physically directing you to where the juice is
- your child asks for, or directs you to a preferred activity
- your child refuses an undesirable activity verbally, or behaviorally
- you have tried underwear on your child but he or she prefers the feel and familiarity of diapers
- your child hides behind a couch, or other places in your home to eliminate
- your child can follow two-step directions
- your child responds to praise however minimally

- your child responds to your voice, or certain noises
- your child responds differently to environmental changes.

Why should you potty train your child?

The second question to answer in the use of the Individualized Teaching approach is the question of why you should potty train your child. Our children with developmental disorders encounter a variety of challenges that can prove to be daunting to parents and educators. As parents and teachers, we are faced with behavior, health, and/or communication issues that seem to take precedence over potty training, and prioritizing our children's needs can become an overwhelming task. Very often, potty training is the last skill that we think of implementing, and by the time we are confronted with potty training our children, they have learned potty behaviors that, because of the passage of time, have become ingrained in their repertoire of behaviors, making potty training a very difficult process. The major reason to potty train your child is to facilitate independence. Potty training *is* the beginning of the road to independence. When I consult with parents and teachers of children with special needs, independence skills training is at the top of the list. I know that teaching my son to become independent across different areas has been and will always be my driving force. In my own personal experience as a mother of a child with special needs, I knew that potty training was a skill that I needed to tackle, and tackle quickly, in order to increase my son's opportunities for future independence.

Alex potty trained at age two. At the beginning, it was a difficult task for me to undertake until I developed Ready, Set, Potty! I could not believe that it only took three days to help him achieve this important skill, when I had tried so many other approaches only to end up frustrated and very discouraged. I believe that a good potty training system should involve a strong motivating factor for both children and parents. For my son, I infused within the potty training process a strong motivator that we will discuss later, and for me, my motivating factor was his entrance into independence, and the things that I could buy for myself with the money that I would save in diapers. Before I attempted to help my son potty train, I noticed the tremendous amount of money spent in buying diapers, and during the potty training process, I decided to reward myself with that money for a year, and actually saved quite a bit to pamper myself every now and then.

For how long should I try a potty training system?

Finally, the question of how long you should hold on to a potty training program is an important question to address. When potty training a child with developmental disorders, consider that every time you start and stop any potty training program, you are setting the process back by six months. This is not to say that if you have attempted to potty train your child twice in the past, it will take a year to successfully potty train him or her. What it means is that for any skill that you teach and have to re-teach, it takes about six months for the child to dispose of the skills previously learned, and substitute the old knowledge with the new learning. This is why it is very important to have a goal and a plan when teaching our children to acquire skills. I recommend that if after a week of trying a new potty training system you do not see *any* progress at all, then the system itself has to be re-evaluated, not substituted.

In potty training your child, you must ask yourself if the information you are presenting your child with is strong in the type of structure that involves order, predictability, and routine. You must evaluate if the manner in which you are presenting the information to your child includes consistency, clear instructions, and relevance to your child's unique needs, and finally, you must look at the individualization aspect of the program that you are using. Assuming that your child is able to communicate with you in whatever form he or she uses regarding their other basic needs, you must then ask yourself if you are mentally prepared to help and encourage your child to potty train. If you are ready to potty train your child, then follow me through potty training success. In the chapters that follow, you will find tips and techniques of the Ready, Set, Potty! system; these tips and techniques will help you and your child achieve potty training success.

Tips for parents and teachers

- Understanding that your child needs order, predictability, and routine will help you realize that you, just as your child does, need to adhere to the same principles in order to make sense of your environment.

- Ask yourself: what are the two most important short-term goals you want your child to accomplish?

- In your past potty training approaches, have you clearly communicated to your child your expectations using visual supports, and individualization of skills?

- Write one paragraph defining your own involvement in, and commitment to, your potty training program. Write a time line in regard to your commitment.

- Realize that your child is doing what he or she is supposed to be doing given the disability he or she has, and the training he or she has received. Now ask yourself, are you doing what you are supposed to be doing to relay potty training expectations to your child in a clear and concise manner?

CHAPTER **/5/**

AREAS TO CONSIDER

Issues in potty training

"Why can't my child potty train?"

Often, when we attempt to teach our children a new skill, we do so failing to consider the different issues that might get in the way of our children acquiring the skills that lead to success. This is certainly an area in our potty training program that should be addressed in order to facilitate learning. So what are the factors to consider in implementing a successful potty training system? Before beginning any potty training program, ask yourself the following questions:

1. Can my child be potty trained?

Your child is already trained! Yes, your child is already trained to eliminate in his or her diaper. Your number one task in this area is to teach your child to eliminate in the toilet. Once you have accepted that your child is already trained, you can begin to follow a structured plan to teach your child the appropriate places for eliminating. We will go further into this area in subsequent chapters.

2. Who is responsible for potty training?

Many parents and educators believe that the responsibility for potty training falls exclusively on them, when in reality, the only person responsible for potty training is the child him or herself. If we approach potty training from this frame of mind, then we can accept that our only responsibility for potty training is to make sure that we present the information needed to succeed in potty training in an ordered, predictable, and routine manner. This approach, as previously mentioned, will ensure that our children receive the information that we want to relay to them in a clear and concise manner, thereby reducing anxiety and frustration for both you and your child.

3. Am I ready to assist my child in potty training?

This is an important question to answer, because it will help you, as the trainer, alleviate existing anxieties regarding the potty training process. Your readiness to commit to a potty training program is as important as your child's readiness to engage in a potty training program.

4. Is my child ready to be potty trained?

Absolutely! Your child is a very capable being, eager to learn new skills. As his or her potty training coach, it is imperative for you to learn to listen to your child's non-verbal behavior, in order to facilitate and successfully implement a program that can help you achieve your number one goal: guiding your child to potty train as independently as possible.

5. What is my role in the potty training process?

In my workshop presentations, parents and educators often ask about their role in the potty training process, and the answer to this question is simple. Going back to the belief that we are only responsible for our own bodies, then your role in the process is that of an encourager, a motivational entity, a coach, and a cheerleader. Knowing this takes a tremendous amount of pressure off your shoulders, and encourages you to become more creative and proactive during the potty training process.

6. For how long will you commit yourself to the potty training process, how committed will you be in times of stress and frustration, and what are you committed to: the process, or the event?

Answering these questions will help you as a parent, or a teacher of children with special needs, stick to your potty training program by reminding yourself that potty training is not an event; rather, it is a process, a process that will yield the type of success that you expect. You must be physically, mentally, and emotionally ready to assist your child in potty training success, and your readiness lies in your commitment to the process. Remember, there is no room for failure; the only option is to succeed.

7. Why is potty training so hard?

Potty training presents significant difficulties for parents and teachers of children with special needs because we fail to appreciate the following facts:

- Potty training is a learned behavior. From the beginning of our children's lives—when they are newborns—we encourage and applaud their actions, which we should do of course. Feeding and diapering times are *the* most social times between a child and his or her caregiver. We praise our children from the time they are newborns until about the age of two for eliminating in their diaper, and we even come up with cute names for the "product." Then one day, unexpectedly in our children's perception, we change the rules for no apparent reason, by telling them that it is time to pee pee in the toilet. Essentially, what we are telling our children is, "Guess what? You have been doing it wrong all this time, and now you have to go potty in that hole—the toilet." This statement is not to say that we should not encourage our children, or interact with them during diapering times. This statement is to make us aware of the difficulty involved in potty training our children with developmental disorders.

- Potty training is so difficult, because the process denotes that we must meet the expectations of other people. Just think about the last time you attempted to potty train your child. If you are like most of us, you probably told everyone around you that you were going to potty train your child, you told everyone except...your child! From that point forward, well-meaning family members began to ask how you were doing in potty training your child. Soon after, the process changed from the original goal of potty training little Peter, to making sure that you potty train him because everyone is watching.

- Finally, potty training is so difficult because of the anxiety of failure. What if you don't succeed? What would that say about you as a parent? What will you do if this does not work? All these feelings are very legitimate, and at times justified, but know that failure exists only in the absence of learning, and every attempt, whether big or small, gets you closer and closer to your goal.

We have just discussed the different areas that pave the way to a successful potty training program. These areas when considered are important in that they help caregivers of children with developmental disorders recognize thinking patterns, attitudes, and expectations, and help us to adjust behaviors that may interfere with our children successfully acquiring potty training skills. Once we recognize and consider our attitudes, thoughts, and patterns in regard to potty training, our own defense mechanism is lowered, giving way to less anxiety on our part, and resulting in developing and implementing an individualized, and well-structured approach to ensure that our children achieve success. Potty training is the beginning of the journey towards independence for you and your child, so if you are ready to embark on an exciting journey, lets get Ready, Set, Potty!

Tips for parents and teachers

- What has been the single most pressing obstacle in helping your child potty train?

- What are two strategies that you will rely upon in times of frustration during your potty training program?

- What, or who, will your support system be during the potty training process?

- Which of your behaviors/attitudes will you have to adjust in order to facilitate your child's potty training process?

- What are the three most fun/exciting things you could do as a family if your child was potty trained?

CHAPTER 6

THE POTTY PLAN

The importance of planning

"I want to start potty training my son again, but where do I begin?"

A plan without a goal is just a wish, and wishes are unrealized dreams. When I speak to parents and teachers about potty training skills, my number one priority is the child, and my goal is to share with parents and teachers proven techniques to help their children to successfully potty train. Those of us who have or serve children with developmental disorders, do not have the luxury of time on our side. Every day, every hour, every minute may make the difference between institution and independence, and this is why it is critical to begin the process of independence as early as possible. You might be asking yourself if it is truly important to develop a goal for your potty training program. Developing a goal to potty train your child is a priority in achieving potty training success. The concept of developing a potty training goal with objectives has an immediate and lasting impact on the skills we attempt to teach our children with developmental disorders. We need to isolate and understand the goal and intermediate objectives that will help us reach our main goal: potty training our child.

It is imperative that we arm ourselves, not only with information regarding our children's unique modes of learning, but also with knowledge that encompasses an eclectic approach to help us reach our goal. Our children, as stated before, are more like us than they are different: this is a statement that I always keep in mind when teaching students with special needs new skills. When I was working on my Masters degree, my professors would provide me with a syllabus of the course that I was about to take; this syllabus became my road map to fulfill the university's expectations of me as the student. The syllabus was *the* most important document for me, because in it, I would see what the goal of the class was, as well as the objectives that would help me understand the steps necessary to accomplish the stated goal with success. The closer I followed the objectives stated in the course syllabus, the greater my chances were in successfully completing my course. Designing a well-thought-out plan that involves a goal and objective for potty training provides a road map for parents to achieve a desired outcome. In essence, the successful outcome of a plan necessitates a goal, which becomes the targeted outcome, and objectives, which become the tools that facilitate the outcome.

So one of the first and most important things to do once you have decided to potty train your child is to design a plan to achieve your goal. I am not talking about long-ranged goals, for those will emerge as our children grow and develop. I am speaking of a short-term, functional goal with objectives that will help your child understand what is expected of him or her during the potty training process. To develop a proactive goal with functional objectives, it is of utmost importance to know your child's needs. To be clear, I am referring to your child's needs, not your expectations. Your child has a need to become more independent, to be understood, to understand his or her surroundings, and to be encouraged. Your child has a need to communicate their needs/wants, and he or she has the right to reach their full potential. The development of a potty training goal and objectives will help you, as a parent or teacher, focus on specific and relevant information needed to help your child achieve success. A successful plan of action calls for considering your child's individual needs, wants, likes, and dislikes. Once you have isolated these areas, you can move on to developing your potty training goal and objectives. Let's look at an example of developing a potty training goal with objectives.

Setting a goal and objectives: Rodney

Rodney is a 12-year-old boy who is non-verbal and not yet potty trained. Every time the issue of going to the bathroom arises, Rodney becomes frustrated and refuses to co-operate. His anxiety about going to the bathroom often leads to aggressive behaviors, and extreme meltdowns, leaving his mother discouraged and frustrated as well. Rodney's mother reports that Rodney has difficulty with transitioning from one environment to the next. She reports that Rodney likes ceiling fans, and looking at family photographs, especially photographs of one of his siblings, and that he strongly dislikes certain colors such as neon green. I visited Rodney's house to help his mother design a potty training program for him, and I was able to observe some things that I felt kept Rodney from successfully potty training.

- Rodney needed to have a structured home environment that would facilitate his learning, and help him respond to expectations. The lack of order, predictability, and routine offended Rodney's perceptual system, forcing his defense mechanism to come up with his own structure in order to make sense of his environment.

- Rodney was asked to go to the bathroom only after every meal, and he quickly learned what to do to keep himself from going to the bathroom. Rodney had learned that if he took his time completing his meal, maybe, just maybe, his mother would give up, and this actually happened more often than not.

- Once Rodney's mom managed to get him to the bathroom door, Rodney would close his eyes and begin to kick his mother: another internal defense that usually worked well for him. In observing Rodney's aggression in the rest-room, I was able to notice that the shower curtain had some neon green designs; they were small designs, almost invisible to the average person, but to Rodney, they were real threats.

After observation and evaluation of Rodney's environmental responses, his mother and I developed a goal as a plan, and objectives as steps, to successfully design a plan that would lower Rodney's anxiety. We developed a plan that would help clarify Rodney's expectations in regard to potty training, while at the same time facilitating the ultimate goal: helping him achieve potty training success. The first and most important goal that needed to be addressed in Rodney's case was to get him to walk into the restroom without a meltdown. In this case, potty training was the goal, and the objectives served as strategies to lower Rodney's defenses and anxiety about walking into the bathroom. Take a look at the goal and objectives developed for Rodney's potty training system.

Goal

Rodney's parents will develop and implement a successful potty training plan using the principles of Individualized Teaching to help Rodney achieve success and independence in the area of potty training.

Objectives

1. Develop and implement a picture/word schedule to help Rodney establish a routine in his daily activities, and to help him become independent in self-help skills such as grooming, dressing, bathing, and potty training: *routine*.

2. Create age-appropriate and relevant potty training stories designed to increase Rodney's understanding of potty training expectations: *predictability*.

3. Use positive visual behavior supports, such as pictures communicating the sequence in which Rodney is expected to perform the skills, along with relevant, individualized potty training stories to teach desired behaviors in the area of potty training: *order, predictability, and routine*.

4. Use highly motivating and rewarding agents, such as Rodney's favorite dinosaur book as a motivator, and potato chips as Rodney's reward food item, to promote the desired behavior: *order, predictability, and routine*.

5. Discuss ongoing progress, and brainstorm any needed modifications with Rodney's teachers and behavior consultant to assist Rodney in achieving potty training independence within the home, school, and community.

> This objective provided Rodney's mother with opportunities to continuously evaluate Rodney's potty training program, and make adjustments if necessary, rather than abandoning the potty training program.

As you can see, the development of a potty training goal becomes necessary for our children to successfully potty train, while giving parents a road map that will lower their own anxiety about the potty training process. What should your potty training goal be? Potty training should not always be the goal. If the child has difficulty even sitting on the potty, the goal would be to address this issue before addressing the overall potty training goal. If, for example, a child has difficulty even walking into the restroom, walking into the restroom should be addressed before we tackle potty training issues. If the child is stressed over even walking into the restroom, then potty training will be nearly impossible, and this is the major reason why many parents have not experienced success in their previous potty training attempts. Ready, Set, Potty! will guide you through its systematic approach to potty training your child, and will give you specific guidelines and strategies to implement a successful program. It is very important to remember the potty training chain that was previously discussed. Likewise, it is important for us as parents and teachers of children with developmental disorders to be able to visualize the steps necessary to potty train our children. If you are ready, let's begin!

Tips for parents and teachers

- How important is it to write a goal for your potty training program?
- When you write your potty training goal with objectives, make sure that your goal is measurable, and that the objectives provide the vehicle to reach that goal.

- What will the development of a potty training goal do for you as the trainer?

- How will a measurable potty training goal facilitate the outcome?

- What two challenges do you think might result in frustration for you during your potty training program?

THE BEGINNING
OF THE PROCESS

The end will lead us

"This is it. I've made up my mind. My son will potty train, but where do I begin?"

The best place to begin to potty train your child with special needs is at the end. That's right, start at the end! How can starting potty training at the end be possible or even feasible? Well, you have already started at the end by observing, and organizing your child's pyramid of needs and wants, which lead you to write a goal with objectives. You cannot begin the program until you have worked out exactly what must be done at each step, and know clearly why you are doing it; at this point you are Ready. You must then follow up with any necessary preparation in order to be Set. Only then can you start to potty train: Ready, Set, Potty!

Take this as an example. Visualize yourself taking a class in which you are required to write a final report on geography. It would be humanly impossible to write a report without first researching the subject or at the very least reading your text. At the *end* of reading your textbook, you feel that you have gathered enough information to successfully *begin* to write your report, and you have only succeeded to this point by visualizing the end and doing the necessary preparation.

Ready, Set, Potty! operates under the same premise: potty training your child with special needs begins at the end. You must be clear as to what your objectives are before you begin, so that you can work through them to accomplish your goal.

The Ready, Set, Potty! system is made up of 17 steps that must be followed sequentially and simultaneously, in order to achieve success.

Ready, Set, Potty! steps to potty training

The steps are:

1. Pick a target day

2. Establish a baseline

3. Pick a theme

4. Decorate the bathroom and bathroom door

5. Make diapers a thing of the past

6. Decorate your child's underwear

7. List your child's favorite motivators

8. Celebrate the night before

9. Use footprints

10. The toilet seat

11. Create a behavior strip

12. Use a bathroom basket

13. Give a reward

14. Create a potty story

15. Use a first/then chart

16. Bowel movements

17. Night training

In the pages that follow, we will explore the steps to potty training in detail. Do not attempt to start the program until you have read about all the steps and planned how you will carry out each one; this is an important part of planning a well-structured program. One of the most important aspects of any potty training program is to make sure that when potty training a child, parents and teachers, and anyone involved in that child's life, understands and participates in the program, in order to help the child generalize the skills learned from one environment to the next. Generalization of skills is important to ensure that our children succeed, and success can only be achieved through both parents' and teachers' involvement and collaboration. Ready, Set, Potty! will guide parents and teachers through a potty training program that involves order, predictability, and routine. This program will clearly define the reasons and uses for every step involved in the potty training program. It will give you specific examples of how this program can be implemented, and will give you important strategies on how to develop your own program. The most common questions in regard to potty training will be addressed later on in this book, and there will be a general tips for parents and teachers section.

The checklist on pp.118–122 can be used to make notes on your program so that you can structure your plan and share it with any other adults who will be involved in your potty training program. You can then gather the equipment you need to do any preparation that will ensure you are Set. Only then, once you have finished reading this book and completed all of your preparation, should you implement the Ready, Set, Potty! program.

Important note: all the steps in the Ready, Set, Potty! system must be followed sequentially and simultaneously in order to achieve success.

Tips for parents and teachers

- How will considering the end of where your child is in the potty training process facilitate the achievement of your goal?
- Where is the end in regard to your child's lack of potty training skills?
- What are your child's areas of strength and deficit?
- What are *your* areas of strength and deficit in the area of potty training?
- What aspects of your child's areas of strengths do you think will be useful in helping him or her to successfully potty train?

CHAPTER

STEPS TO POTTY TRAINING

1. Pick a target day

More often than not, those of us who want to potty train our children have a date in mind. Having a date to begin your potty training program is a good thing, but often, we pick a potty training date without a plan of action. There are days and times of the year that are easier to potty train children with developmental disorders than others are. Knowing the appropriate times and days to begin a potty training system with your child will make it easier for you as a parent and/or teacher to plan for eventualities, and to increase your chances of success.

In my years of experience in potty training children with special needs, I have found that the best times for potty training are during the Thanksgiving and Christmas holidays. The worst time to potty train is during the summer months. There are two reasons why these two times increase or decrease your chance of success in potty training your child. First, during the holidays, there are so many changes in our children's daily routine, and any well-structured program that you introduce will appeal to your child's need for routine. The second reason why it is easier to potty train during the holidays is that during the cold months, our bodies retain less moisture, making our elimination times more consistent. This is also the reason why potty training in the summer months becomes more of a challenge. During the hot summer months, our bodies retain more moisture than usual, which results in our elimination times changing. This concept does not only apply to children with developmental disorders, but to all of us in general.

Do you ever wonder why the majority of us choose Mondays for the most part to begin something? If you think back to the times when you have decided to stop smoking, lose weight, try a new hobby that you know would be challenging for you, or all of the above, we tend to want to start on a Monday. Mondays are *the* worst days to begin a potty training system. Mondays denote the beginning of the week, the time to pick up something you left undone, the beginning of hard work, and some level of frustration for us parents and teachers. Mondays are usually expected to be busy, hectic, and demanding, due to the weekend that we just left behind. This is the reason why you seldom hear people say, "I can't wait till Monday to go back to work," or "Thank God it's Monday." In potty training my son, I chose the Tuesday before Thanksgiving as my target potty training date. Starting on Tuesday gave Alex the opportunity to experience the potty training system both at school, and at home, while giving me the opportunity to plan, and mentally prepare myself to help Alex succeed. Another day that has worked quite well for potty training is Wednesday. Wednesday is seen as "hump" day, a day that we psychologically prepare ourselves for the much-awaited weekend break from work or school, this is the day when our energy begins to rise in expectation of the break that is to come. It is advisable to pick your target day carefully, taking into consideration the amount of support that you will need, and whether or not you have fully prepared your plan to implement the Ready, Set, Potty! program for your child. Once you have chosen your potty training target day, you must make diapers a thing of the past, with the exception of bedtime. This will be discussed in more detail in this section, but for now, let's look at some samples and tips for picking your target day.

Choosing a target day: Molly

Molly is a three-year-old child whose parents attempted to potty train three times in the past with no success. Molly's mother decided to begin to potty train her during Molly's summer break, since Molly would be out of school for two months. During those two months, Molly and her family had so many summer activities that it became difficult to establish a routine, and almost impossible to establish any type of consistent schedule. Although Molly's parents developed a potty training goal, which gave them a guideline to potty train Molly, the lack of order, predictability, and routine in Molly's daily activities yielded poor potty training results, and her parents aborted their potty training efforts within two days, thinking that Molly was not ready to be potty trained. Molly *was* ready to be potty trained, and her parents followed most of the steps in her potty training program, except picking a target day and time of the year that would give Molly the highest probability of success. As a result of this, Molly was unable to internalize the skills needed to potty train. Four months after the last potty training attempt, Molly's parents chose to begin their potty training program on a Wednesday in October. Molly took to her potty training quickly; she was potty trained in one week.

Choosing a target day: Joseph

Joseph's parents had been trying to potty train him for the past 12 years with no success. Now 15 years old, Joseph was still not potty trained, and his parents were extremely frustrated about the process, thinking that Joseph would never be independent with his potty training skills. Joseph's parents chose to potty train him during Spring Break, since his grandparents were going to be visiting; they thought an extra set of hands would be helpful during the potty training process. Three days into their potty training attempt, they aborted the mission because Joseph became very unfocused and uncooperative. The problem was that having new visitors in the home at the time that Joseph's parents implemented their potty training program broke Joseph's order, predictability, and routine, which resulted in an imbalance of his home structure. Furthermore, Joseph's grandparents did not have the same expectations that his parents had, and did not help in providing the consistency that Joseph needed, because they had other ideas on how to potty train Joseph. Joseph's grandparents helped his parents to a certain degree, but they also skipped some of the steps in Joseph's potty training program thinking that some of the steps were not necessary.

Choosing a target day: Alex

Alex's parents decided to potty train him during the Thanksgiving break. In planning for the implementation of the potty training program, they communicated with Alex's teachers about the program that they would be using. Alex's parents met with his teachers to explain the potty training program, and requested his teachers' involvement to help Alex succeed. Not only did Alex's parents enlist the help of his teachers, but they also carefully explained Alex's potty training plan, and worked closely with his teachers to develop and implement the plan at school as well. Alex's potty training program began the Tuesday before the Thanksgiving break. This approach facilitated Alex's generalization of skills between the home, and the school environment. Both Alex's teachers, and his parents, followed the same potty training program using the same strategies, which provided Alex with order, predictability, and routine across different environments, and the result was immediate; Alex potty trained in three days!

Tips for parents and teachers

- Do not attempt to begin to potty train on a Monday; this will increase your and your child's anxiety.

- You should not overly restrict your normal activities, but if you will be having visitors, just make sure that they follow your potty training program, and that they adhere as closely as possible to your potty training plan.

- Do not attempt to potty train during the summer months. The lack of structure due to various summer activities will break your child's order, predictability, and routine. Furthermore, our bodies retain more fluids during hot weather months, and the increase in fluid intake might lead to inconsistency in your child's elimination times.

- Avoid carbonated/caffeinated clear liquids and apple juice; these types of beverages change our body's natural elimination schedule. Do not increase or decrease fluid intake; doing so will unbalance your child's elimination times.

- Any potty training program should be developed and implemented by both the school and the home environment to facilitate generalization of skills from one environment to the next.

- Be ready to experience success; potty training your child is right around the corner!

2. Establish a baseline

It is important to determine your child's potty pattern, or the time of the day that your child wets him or herself; this can be done by establishing a baseline. In order to establish a baseline, you must check your child, and then offer him or her the opportunity to go to the toilet every 45 minutes to an hour, depending on the type of information you have gathered from your baseline. By charting your child's elimination times, you will help him or her become more aware of the need to eliminate. The information gathered through the baseline will also help you establish what times to encourage toilet or potty use. Your child will typically have more liquids in his or her body during the early part of the day. Therefore, the ideal time to offer opportunities to go to the toilet is during the early part of the day, and first thing in the morning. If your child normally gets up at 8:00 in the morning, wake him or her up 15 minutes earlier: at 7:45. This is what I call the backtrack rule. This strategy will provide a better chance of eliminating in the toilet successfully. Thereafter, direct your child to go to the toilet every 45 minutes to an hour, but always keep in mind that you need to backtrack 15 minutes from your stated baseline times.

Please be aware that your child will have the most accidents during the first day of the potty training process this is very common even for neuro-typical children. Remember that your child is trying to assimilate the new information that you are introducing him or her to. Do not be discouraged by potty accidents. The more accidents your child experiences on the first day of potty training, the more opportunities you will have to teach him or her the difference between wet and dry, and this repetition provides the basis for the internalization of the potty training skills. Table 8.1 illustrates a sample potty training baseline, which is the actual baseline that I developed for Alex. You can create your own or use the blank version given in Table 8.2. Again, keep in mind that all the steps in the Ready, Set, Potty! system must be followed sequentially and simultaneously in order to achieve success.

Table 8.1 gives a clear example of what a potty training baseline should look like. One of the most important aspects in establishing a baseline is to keep in mind that potty accidents will occur, and if we view accidents as opportunities, they can provide parents and teachers with information as to a child's elimination times. A baseline will communicate to you if there are any adjustments that need to be made to your potty training program, and how close your child is to experiencing potty training success. In my potty training experience with my son, my baseline indicated to me that I needed to take Alex to the restroom six times per day: in the morning at 7:30, 9:00, and 11:00. Alex's afternoon potty times were at 2:45, 6:15, and 7:10 approximately. Please keep in mind that the elimination times that your baseline provides are approximate times of when your child is more likely to eliminate when taken to the restroom. Give or take five or ten minutes, use your baseline to increase your child's probability of success when going to the potty. Let's look at some examples of the importance of developing a baseline.

Establishing a baseline: Jackson

Bren's biggest potty training challenge was to discern, and isolate, the exact times when her son needed to go to the bathroom. To Bren, it seemed as though Jackson's elimination times were all the time! Bren believed that Jackson urinated very inconsistently, and as a result, she was not able to isolate specific times to take him to the toilet. Jackson was still on diapers and was offered to go to the toilet several times a day with no success. Bren soon grew frustrated with her potty training program and decided to try one last thing: to isolate the times that Jackson was likely to eliminate. In order to isolate the approximate times Jackson was more likely to eliminate, Bren developed an elimination chart. This elimination chart gave Bren average times of elimination, and once those times were isolated, Jackson began to make a connection between what was expected of him, and his actions, which resulted in potty training success. This is what I call a prime example of internalization of skills.

Using underwear instead of diapers to establish a baseline: Emily

Emily was in diapers during the potty training process. Her parents tried to take her to the potty several times a day unsuccessfully, and were very frustrated by the failed attempts. Because Emily was in diapers all during the day, her parents were not able to establish a baseline, and quickly gave up the potty training program. It was recommended to them that in order for them to be able to clearly isolate Emily's elimination times, they needed to be aware of Emily's potty accidents the minute they occurred, so that they could intervene proactively, and offer Emily alternatives as to where to eliminate. Emily's parents soon understood that in order to be able to develop their baseline they needed to have Emily wear underwear all throughout the potty training process. This simple step provided Emily's parents with the information they needed as to Emily's elimination times, and allowed them to intervene in a positive way, offering Emily the opportunity to experience success in the potty.

Isolating elimination times: Kyle

Kyle was completely off diapers from the first day of his potty training program. His parents kept detailed information regarding Kyle's elimination times by using a baseline. Their baseline provided them with accurate information as to Kyle's elimination schedule. Once an average baseline was established, Kyle's parents isolated five different potty times throughout the day, knocking off 15 minutes from their established times. This approach yielded the information they needed to increase the chances of potty training success for Kyle. By following this approach, Kyle's parents provided him with opportunities to learn the concept of wet versus dry, and decreased the level of anxiety for Kyle as well as for them.

Tips for parents and teachers

- Establish a consistent baseline for the home and school environment using the same baseline sheet to isolate elimination times.

- Once elimination times have been isolated, deduct 15 minutes from the isolated times to ensure success.

- Do not use diapers or training pants throughout the daytime toilet training process.

- Establish toilet routines to increase your opportunities for success.

- Do not use the baseline as a stand-alone step to potty training your child; the baseline is one link in the potty training chain.

Table 8.1: Alex's baseline

D = Dry pants
W = Wet pants
P = Eliminated in potty
BM = Bowel movement
No = Did not eliminate in potty or pants

Time	Monday		Tuesday		Wednesday		Thursday		Friday		Saturday		Sunday	
	Potty	Pants	Potty	Pants	Potty	Pants	Potty	Pants	Potty	Pants	Potty	Pants	Potty	Pants
*7:45	P	D	No	D	P	D	P	D	P	D	No	D	P	D
8:30	P	D	P	D	P	D	P	D	P	D	P	D	P	D
*9:15	P	D	No	W	No	D	P	D	P	D	P	D	P	D
10:40	No	W	P	D	P	D	P	D	P	D	P	D	P	D
*11:15	P	D	No	D	P	D	P	D	P	D	P	D	P	D
12:30	No	W	P	D	P	D	No	W	P	D	P	D	P	D
1:45	No	W	P	D	No	W	P	D	P	D	P	D	P	D
*2:50	P	D	No	W	P	D	P	D	P	D	P	D	P	D
3:30	No	BM	P	D	P	D	P	D	P	D	P	D	P	D
4:15	P	D	P	D	P	D	P	D	P	D	P	D	P	D
*6:30	P	D	No	W	P	D	P	D	P	D	P	D	P	D
*7:25	P	D	P	D	P	D	P	D	P	D	P	D	P	D
Total	P = 8	W = 3	P = 7	W = 3	P = 10	W = 1	P = 11	W = 1	P = 12	W = 0	P = 11	W = 0	P = 12	W = 0

* possible elimination times.

Table 8.2: Create your own baseline

D = Dry pants
W = Wet pants
P = Eliminated in potty
BM = Bowel movement
No = Did not eliminate in potty or pants

Time	Monday		Tuesday		Wednesday		Thursday		Friday		Saturday		Sunday	
	Potty	Pants	Potty	Pants	Potty	Pants	Potty	Pants	Potty	Pants	Potty	Pants	Potty	Pants
Total	P =	W =	P =	W =	P =	W =	P =	W =	P =	W =	P =	W =	P =	W =

* possible elimination times.

3. Pick a theme

Picking a theme for your potty training program is a great way to entice your child to use the bathroom. This approach will give your child a valid reason to eliminate in the toilet, it will decrease his or her anxiety in regard to going to the toilet, and picking a theme makes the process of potty training fun for both you and your child. In my years of helping parents and teachers potty train their children with special needs, I have found that in order to help children internalize and generalize potty training skills, the environment must be one that blends familiar and unfamiliar concepts. The blending of these two concepts offers our children a sense of order and predictability, in the presence of unfamiliar expectations.

In my potty training experience with my son, for example, I knew that some of the things that Alex liked most were bright colors, pictures of animals, family vacation photos, and birthday parties. I chose a birthday party theme for my Alex's potty training program knowing how much he enjoyed going to parties. I chose not to use bright colors for my theme, because I knew that some bright colors provided sensory stimulation for Alex, and I needed to keep his attention focus on the task. The theme you choose for your potty training program must also be one that your child can only experience in the bathroom, and in no other room around your house. To illustrate the importance of picking the right theme, I will share some examples with you.

Using a music theme: Patty

Patty is a 16-year-old girl, whose lack of potty training skills has kept her from participating in many activities in and out of school. Her parents have tried just about everything they could think of, but Patty resisted eliminating in the bathroom, and would only eliminate in the hot tub. Patty's parents reported that she was unmotivated, and that she did not like anything outside of her music class at school. Her parents had tried to use music in the various potty training programs with little success. I visited Patty's house in order to find out what the root of the problems was, and indeed, Patty seemed unmotivated, but I noticed Patty forming musical notes with a string. This type of behavior prompted me to think about picking large, plastic music notes posted on the bathroom's wall as Patty's potty training theme, and we saw immediate success once this concept was instituted into her potty training program.

Using a birthday party theme: Alex

I knew that in order to help Alex become successful in potty training, I needed to find a potty training theme that would give him a good enough reason to eliminate in the potty. I chose a birthday party theme for my potty training program. I made sure to stay away from real balloons, as this would entice him to get off the potty to touch them; instead, I used balloon cutouts, birthday party hats, whistles, and birthday party photographs. I refrained from using anything that had bright colors, because bright colors generally made Alex hyperactive, and decreased his attention span. Every time Alex asked for a balloon, I would take him to the bathroom and have him sit on the potty; this facilitated my potty training program, and Alex was able to potty train with very little effort, because he saw relevance in our expectations.

Using a Christmas tree theme: Jason

Jason had a fascination with Christmas trees, so for the past three or four years, Jason's mother would wait until the month of December to potty train him. Jason was already eight years old and not yet potty trained. His mother was frustrated and could not understand why if she used the Christmas theme for Jason's potty training program, he was not successful in potty training. One of the major problems with Jason's potty training theme was that by taking advantage of the Christmas season, Jason had access to Christmas trees everywhere he went, so Jason's motivation to go to the toilet was low. He did not have to eliminate in the potty to see a Christmas tree; he could see one just by walking into his living room. Keeping this in mind, we postponed Jason's potty training program until the month of March after not seeing Christmas trees for a while, the introduction of his favorite theme lowered his anxiety, and provided the needed visual stimulation, and motivation for Jason to become successfully potty trained in one week.

Tips for parents and teachers

- Pick a theme that reflects your child's favorite activity, character, or color.

- Make sure that your theme provides the proper visual stimulation.

- Do not use your chosen theme in any other area of your house/classroom.

- Make sure your theme is well balanced, with familiar and unfamiliar concepts.

- Make sure that your chosen theme does not over-stimulate your child's senses.

- Your theme has to be of high appeal to your child, and your child has to see relevance in it, this will help decrease his or her anxiety about going to the bathroom.

4. Decorate the bathroom and bathroom door

We all have our own styles of decorating our surroundings, and we do so keeping in mind our personalities, our likes, our dislikes, and our comfort. Our children are more like us than they are different. Think of all the stores that specialize in selling bathroom décor, and think about the amount of money that one can spend in decorating just one bathroom. Now, ask yourself this question: why do you spend so much money to decorate *your* bathroom, and why do you decorate your bathroom? The answer to this question is easy. We decorate our bathrooms because bathrooms are boring!

In the previous section, we discussed the importance of picking a potty theme, and the decorating of your bathroom is where your potty theme comes into play. Your child needs a reason to do something different other than what he or she is used to doing. Your child, just like you, needs to be in a secure, familiar, and pleasant environment in order to feel comfortable in the face of unfamiliarity. Keeping your potty theme in mind, isolate and decorate the bathroom that you intend to use during your potty training program. You only need to decorate one bathroom, so choose a bathroom that is easily accessible from the main area of your house. Easy accessibility will minimize potty accidents, and will make it easier for you to be able to monitor your child during the potty training process.

My decorations during Alex's potty training process included balloons, pictures of Alex, birthday cards, and party hats posted on the walls of the bathroom. I made sure that my decorations were not at Alex's eye level to keep him from tearing them off the walls. It is important to decorate the bathroom the night before you begin your potty training program. It is advisable to do so at the time when your child is already in bed so he or she will be surprised when they see it. One of the reasons why this approach works so well as part of the potty training process is because the element of surprise will divert your child's attention from his or her anxiety over using the restroom. I also suggest that you post a picture of a toilet seat on the outside of your bathroom door; visual cues help our children internalize new concepts, because these cues give our children access to the information they need, when they need it.

Decorating the bathroom: Joel

Joel's favorite person in the world is his grandmother and he loves his grandmother's bedroom, where he spends a significant amount of time when they visit her. Joel's father used pictures of the different rooms in his grandmother's house as Joel's potty theme to decorate the bathroom. Joel's grandmother lived out of town, so the opportunities for Joel to visit were minimal. Knowing how much Joel likes visiting his grandmother, Joel's father took pictures of his grandmother sitting in different rooms in her house greeting Joel. The pictures that called to Joel's attention the most were the pictures of his grandmother's bedroom, so those pictures were strategically placed on the bathroom's wall that Joel would be facing when sitting on the toilet seat. This strategy helped to stop Joel's constant getting up, and kept him focused while sitting on the seat.

Decorating the bathroom and using music: Roma

Roma's parents knew that she enjoyed classical music and opera, but were unable to isolate what it was about that particular genre of music that she liked so much. Upon examination of her choices in music, they were able to isolate a particular artist that she enjoyed the most, and realized that it was not the music, but the singer's voice that provided serenity and focus when Roma listened to his music. Keeping Roma's interest in mind, her parents gathered several pictures of the opera singer she liked, and decorated the bathroom with those pictures. Roma's parents also added a CD with some of the artist's songs, therefore giving Roma the much-needed visual and auditory stimulation to lower her defenses regarding potty training skills.

Finding the motivator and decorating the bathroom: Mira

It is not too late to begin potty training your child with a developmental disorder. If your potty training program involves order, predictability, and routine, coupled with consideration of your child's sensory issues, potty training is possible at any age. Mira was a 17-year-old young lady, who was not yet potty trained, and on the surface, showed no interest in potty training. Just like most typical teenagers, Mira's motivation was low. After years of trying different potty training programs and approaches, her parents had all but given up on the prospect of potty training her. Mira was non-verbal, and on the surface seemed very uninterested in her surroundings at home. In talking to Mira's parents and teachers, and visiting her home and her school, I discovered that there was one important motivator that had gone unnoticed by everyone in Mira's life. The only time Mira seemed interested and connected to her environment was when she would walk down one of the school's hallways at a certain class period. In following Mira around the school for a couple of days, I noticed her particular interest in one classroom. Every time Mira was in that hallway, she would walk towards this particular class, and peek into the classroom three consecutive times. She would then resume her walk down the hallway with a smile on her face.

What was it that was of so much interest, and that brought Mira such pleasure? I asked her to show me what she was thinking about, and she rubbed her shoulders up and down, then flipped her pony tail and laughed. Her cues were not clear to me, so I decided to sit in that class, and have Mira's teacher walk her down the hall again. Mira stopped by the classroom, looked in a definite direction, and went through her daily ritual. It was then that it hit me; Mira's motivation was a male student, who had broad shoulders and a ponytail, and who could blame her, he was indeed motivating to look at!

The biggest challenge was not to potty train Mira, but to convince this student to allow me to take pictures of him to potty train someone. After much, much convincing, he agreed to be photographed, and this is what Mira's parents used as the theme to decorate her bathroom. Blessings come in different fashions: Mira potty trained in two weeks and quickly acquired other motivations; our student model is in college majoring in Special Education, and eager to begin his journey of helping students with special needs succeed.

Tips for parents and teachers

- Choose your bathroom's decorations wisely to avoid sensory overload do not over-decorate.

- Assess your child's likes and dislikes, and ensure that your decoration theme provides your child with sufficient motivation to go to the toilet.

- Communication between the home and the school environment is imperative to ensure that you are catering to your child's unique needs.

- Decorate only one bathroom in the house.

- At school, teachers can put together a potty bag that contains the motivating items for the student they are trying to potty train to take to the bathroom if the classroom does not have a private bathroom.

- Make sure that your child does not have access to the theme you are using other than in the bathroom this will encourage him or her to go to the bathroom with the minimal amount of stress.

5. Make diapers a thing of the past

We expect our children to understand and internalize potty training expectations from the moment we put them in regular underwear. Let us remember that regular underwear is made from very different material than pull-up type diapers or training pants, and if your child has sensory issues, they are sure to object to this change. Regular underwear just feels different and as a result, the child's whole focus could be on the feeling of their new underwear rather than what their body is feeling. This is often the reason why, on the first day of potty training, many children will go to look for their diapers; many will even beg for one! We expect our children to let us know when they want to go to the bathroom; we expect them to understand that they should never wet their underwear again the minute we begin our attempt to potty train them. If you look at it from your child's point of view, the motivation for him or her is not great, the reason is simply not good enough, and in their mode of thinking, why change something that has been working just fine for them?

Wearing diapers is the equivalent of carrying your very own personal potty with you at all times, and using diapers during the potty training process confuses the child as to when and where it is appropriate to eliminate, and prevents him or her from being able to tell the difference between wet and dry. To be clear, making diapers a thing of the past means no diapers, no pull-ups, training pants, or plastic overpants.

The notion of giving up diapers completely produces more anxiety for parents and teachers than for the child who is being potty trained, because of the many accidents that the child will have on the first day of the potty training program. There *will* be accidents, this is common and should be expected. Remember, your child is learning a totally new concept, and new skills to pair up with that concept, in order to modify his or her behavior to your expectations: a behavior that has been displayed for three, five, and in some cases 15 years. Reverting to the use of diapers will only delay the potty training process. A diaper can be used only at night, and only right before bedtime, preferably after your child has fallen asleep. Putting a diaper on your child while he or she is awake would prompt your child to hold his or her eliminations until bedtime. Use white cotton underwear for boys and nylon panties for girls. The white cotton underwear for boys will make it easier for the child to be visually aware of the wet spot, while at the same time will concentrate his efforts more on keeping the figure that the parents have drawn on his underwear dry. In addition, boys wet in the front and, when so, their underwear does not adhere to the front as it would if they were to wet in the back, which is the case with girls. Girls wet in the back and for this reason the wet spot is closer to their skin. This, coupled with the fact that cotton retains heat more than nylon does close to the body, means that cotton underwear for girls will keep the wet spot closer to their bodies making it difficult for them to be able to get the feeling of being wet. These types of materials are thin enough to help your child increase his or her awareness of wet versus dry, while at the same time helping you, as the trainer, become more aware of your child's elimination times, giving you opportunities to intervene before they eliminate.

Making diapers a thing of the past: Bren

Bren's parents had decided to potty train her during the Fall Break. They gathered all the materials necessary to individualize her potty training program and were determined to succeed this time. While the majority of the potty training steps were followed, Bren's parents decided to use diapers only when on outings. Bren had therapy outside of her home on a daily basis, so her mother would use a diaper for the car ride to avoid accidents. Soon Bren learned to hold her elimination until she had her diaper on, and she learned that this would happen before getting in the car. Bren's parents were very frustrated by her elimination times, and could not understand why it was that Bren would wait to eliminate until she got in the car. In Bren's case, the use of a diaper at specific times sent her body signals to eliminate only while wearing a diaper, which is something she was familiar with, and a behavior that was part of her for eight years. Once Bren's parents understood that they were sending Bren mixed signals by alternating between diapers and regular underwear, they were able to understand that making diapers a thing of the past was necessary, in order to help Bren internalize the potty training skills, and use those skills to follow through her potty training expectations.

Making diapers a thing of the past: Jimmy

The first day of potty training was turning out to be chaotic for Jimmy's parents. After many accidents, they just could not understand why Jimmy was not getting it. Jimmy's parents thought they were following his potty training program systematically, but alternated using diapers depending on how many potty accidents Jimmy would have. Jimmy's parents did not get rid of diapers completely; they kept a bag of diapers hidden to be used in "emergencies." Although Jimmy seemed not to understand many concepts according to his parents, he had learned that he would get a diaper sooner or later. After an accident, Jimmy would go to where his parents had the diapers "hidden," and would bring one to his mom. This type of behavior meant that Jimmy knew what to do to get a diaper on, and where to go to get it. I consulted with Jimmy's parents and advised them to get rid of the diapers completely, and to make Jimmy a part of this event, by having him put the bag of diapers in the trash and say, "Bye-bye diapers, diapers are gone." This simple step communicated to Jimmy that diapers were no longer an option, and that wearing underwear was his only choice. After a day of practicing this with Jimmy, his potty accidents decreased by one per day.

Making diapers a thing of the past: Maggie

Maggie's parents decided to make diapers a thing of the past, knowing and expecting that Maggie would have a few accidents at the beginning of her potty training program. Maggie's parents knew that Maggie understood the concepts of something being finished, and of giving something away. Her parents decided to have Maggie give her neighbor, whom Maggie liked a lot, her last bag of diapers. From that point forward, Maggie's parents kept reminding her that she now had underwear *only*, and that the diapers were finished. One day, Maggie saw her neighbor and asked for the diapers, her neighbor followed the same protocol by telling her that the diapers were finished, and that she only had underwear. In this sample, Maggie's parents had reduced her choices, making underwear the only choice. Maggie quickly internalized that information, and stopped asking for diapers. What Maggie's parents did by using this approach was to relate to her that her only choice was to wear her underwear and that diapers were no longer part of her. This facilitated Maggie's potty training process, and she was potty trained in four days with minimal frustration to her parents.

Tips for parents and teachers

- Make diapers a thing of the past from the first day of your potty training program.

- Communicate to the child both visually and verbally that the diapers are gone.

- Involve your child in disposing of all the diapers in the house.

- Make underwear the only choice for your child.

- Do not, under any circumstances, go back to diapers during the day.

- When your child asks for a diaper, use a picture or word to communicate to him or her that underwear is the only option, and do so in a very positive manner pointing out his or her new underwear.

- When your child asks for a diaper, communicate to him or her that pee pee goes in the potty only.

6. Decorate your child's underwear

We all need reasons why we should or should not do something, and your child is no different. If you are asking your child to give up something that means security for him or her, then why should they give that up? Why should they exchange diapers, which are comfortable to them, for underwear, which are unfamiliar and uncomfortable to them? As has been said, our children are more like us than they are different. All of us in giving up something that has been working for us need to know what is in it for us. What will we gain in giving up something that works for us? What is in it for your child? In giving up diapers, you are asking your child to give up something familiar, comfortable, and secure for him or her. Many of us do not think about what we are asking our children to give up when we begin the potty training process. We do not think of this because we have never stopped to think what potty training was like for us. In my many potty training workshops, I ask participants to remember when they were potty trained. The majority of them do not remember the experience, and those who do, do not share it with others. The potty training experience may well have been a very traumatic experience for us, so it may have been erased from our memory, and keeping this in mind will help you understand what your child must be experiencing during his or her potty training program.

If you are asking your child to exchange diapers for underwear, you must include in the exchange something so meaningful and relevant, that it encourages your child to willingly participate in that exchange. One of the ways in which we can facilitate that exchange, and make it relevant to our children, is by decorating the underwear using the potty training theme chosen for your particular potty training program. It is recommended to use white cotton underwear for boys and nylon panties for girls. You will need several pairs of underwear for your potty training program. I bought 12 pairs of regular, white cotton underwear for boys. I decided to decorate them with a theme-related item. Alex loved balloons, particularly blue ones, so I drew a blue balloon on the front of the underwear. I knew Alex liked balloons so much that he would not want to wet his "balloon." Decorating the underwear with a single balloon helped Alex focus on keeping his balloon dry, rather than on the single issue of eliminating in the potty and this decreased his anxiety over what I expected him to do. I talked to Alex about keeping his balloon dry and that pee pee, as we called it, went in the potty only. Alex continually looked at the balloon on his underwear to make sure it was dry; by doing this, he was able to recognize the feeling of needing to urinate. I do not recommend buying underwear that has many designs on it, because your child might feel that since there are so many designs on the underwear, it is OK to wet some of the designs, as long as one stays dry. So be sure that the underwear is white, and that your chosen design is placed on the front of the child's underwear. Drawing Alex's favorite design on the underwear worked wonderfully, because it brought relevance and familiarity to the potty training process.

If your child happens to have an accident, remain calm, and have them touch the front of their underwear where it is wet and remind them, "This is wet; the rule is pee pee goes in the potty only." Next, have your child go to the bathroom to change their clothes. Independence must be encouraged in this activity, even if you have to teach this skill hand-over-hand. Figure 8.1 illustrates an example of the underwear; note where to place the symbol.

Balloon

Figure 8.1: Decorated underwear

Decorating underwear in the wrong place: Mia

Mia's mother knew that Mia liked red triangles, so she decided to buy several pairs of underwear, and paint red triangles all over the underwear. Mia's curiosity was stimulated by the red triangles all over her underwear, particularly the ones on the back of her underwear. Mia began going around in circles in an effort to see the triangles on the back of her underwear. This behavior soon became a problem, because this type of movement over-stimulated Mia's vestibular system, creating an issue of hyperactivity. Mia's over-excitement also made her thirstier than usual, and prompted her to drink excessively changing her elimination times drastically.

Decorating underwear with letters of the alphabet: Preston

Children with special needs understand the concept of beginning and end; the concept of something finishing is important to them, as it is to all of us. One idea when thinking about underwear designs to make potty training relevant to children, is to decorate the underwear with alphabet letters using permanent fabric paint. I have used this approach several times with great results. Placing one letter of the alphabet on the underwear helped Preston to focus on the one and only letter he could see, and he treasured his letter so much, that his focus was on keeping the letter dry, and on getting his next letter by going pee pee in the potty. In this example, the child's motivation for not wetting his underwear was to keep his letter dry, while he was also being motivated to eliminate in the potty to get the underwear that followed the next letter in sequence. This approach communicated to him that in order to get the next letter in the sequence, he had to go pee pee in the potty.

Decorating underwear with a yellow ball: Lee

Lee's fascination with yellow balls was the key to helping him potty train with success. Lee's parents decided to hide every yellow ball that they had in the house a day before beginning their potty training program, and used that concept to decorate his underwear. They painted a yellow ball on the center of Lee's underwear—the crotch—and surprised him with the yellow ball underwear on the first day of potty training. Lee's only access to a yellow ball was the ball painted on his underwear, so in the absence of the actual yellow ball, he took particular interest in the ball on his underwear, and focused on keeping his "yellow ball dry."

Tips for parents and teachers

- Use permanent fabric paint to decorate the underwear. Washable paint may entice your child to eliminate in his or her underwear just to see the design go away.

- Stay away from training pants or pull-ups, as these type of items become warm and can become comfortable when wet, which can delay the potty training process.

- Expect some accidents particularly on the first day of your potty training program. View every potty accident as a step closer to your child understanding what your expectations are.

- Help your child focus on keeping his or her underwear's design dry, rather than eliminating in the potty; this will help minimize your child's anxiety, as well as helping increase awareness of his or her body's elimination signals.

- Remember the number one rule for helping your child to learn a new skill: do as much as possible to help your child learn/understand a concept, but as little as possible in order to encourage independence.

- Teach your child the concepts of wet, dry and cold, by pouring a small amount of apple juice on the underwear when your child is not watching you, and placing the underwear in the freezer for about one to two hours. Sit in a comfortable area on the floor with your child, place the underwear on the floor along with some dry underwear, and show him or her the underwear, guiding his or her hand to touch the wet, then the dry underwear saying: this is wet, this is dry, this is wet, this is dry, show me wet, show me dry. Repeat this exercise until your child responds correctly at least three out of five times. Make sure to reward your child's correct responses with his favorite edible reward. Once your child has responded to your wet/dry samples, have him wear the dry underwear and tell him: this is dry, then follow by the wet sample, making sure it is not still frozen, or too cold, and say: this is wet; pee pee goes in the potty only. Help your child change into the dry underwear, and remind him thereafter to check his "balloon" or other design and take him or her to the toilet.

7. List your child's favorite motivators

As I have said, our children are more like us than they are different. Our children with developmental disorders, much like us, need motivators to encourage them to perform certain activities with success. Sometimes our motivation comes from visualizing the outcome, but in the case of children with developmental disorders, their motivation must be of high interest to them, since delayed gratification has not yet developed in our children. Motivators must be relevant in order for our children to be able to make connections between actions and reactions, and finally, motivators should be of high appeal to them, in order to encourage their engagement.

The use of motivators is a very important component in the Ready, Set, Potty! program. The use of motivators should be individualized to your child's likes and dislikes, in order for them to have a powerful impact on their behavior. Motivators are different from rewards. Motivators are things that you will let your child "borrow" while sitting on the potty; they are continuous in nature, and highly appealing to your child's sense of touch, smell, vision, and/or hearing. These motivators should be placed in a basket near the toilet, and should be available to your child only for as long as he or she is seated on the toilet. The availability of these items in the bathroom is not unique to the special needs population. Walk in any household bathroom, and what do you see? Magazines! Do you ever wonder why people have reading material in bathrooms? Perhaps the answer to this question is because bathrooms are not only boring, but they are also unappealing by nature.

Using motivators in the bathroom during the potty training program works much like us having magazines in the bathroom as reading material; they relax us! When you consider which motivators to use for your child's potty training program, keep in mind items that are of high appeal to your child, which also provide significance, relevance, and sensory stimulation to your child. If you choose five motivating items, make sure that each of these items has at least two sensory components. So choose an item that your child likes the look *and* the feel of; doing this will provide you with ten sensory stimulating items within the five that you have chosen. Some samples of motivators for your Ready, Set, Potty! program might be small picture albums, whistles, books, plastic alphabet letters, and playing your child's favorite music on a CD in the bathroom. Remember to be as creative as you can, and above all, have fun during your potty training program.

Using sensory motivators: Antonio

Antonio's parents were able to isolate their son's elimination times, but still found it challenging to keep him seated on the potty. Antonio's mom would sit right next to him singing songs, but nothing seemed to help, Antonio would refuse to sit on the potty for more than 17 seconds. Antonio's parents had no visual motivators for him, they used verbal motivators as attempts to encourage him to use the potty, but nothing seemed to work, and soon they gave up on their potty training attempt.

What was lacking in Antonio's potty training program was the use of powerful, tangible motivators that would give Antonio a reason to remain seated on the potty, and at the same time relax him enough to achieve potty success. To provide Antonio with the sensory motivation to remain on the potty, his parents used gloves full of rice and beans as motivators. Furthermore, they sewed buttons of different colors on each finger; this is something that helped increase Antonio's focus, because he liked looking at buttons. Antonio understood that he could hold on to the gloves as long as he was seated on the potty. Antonio's motivator served as a relaxing agent for him and soon, Antonio experienced his first successful elimination in the potty.

Using photos and music as motivators: Tia

Tia's potty training program was created with Tia's needs in mind. Her parents designed a potty training program that took into consideration Tia's likes and dislikes, and used this information to creatively design a successful potty training program for her. Tia is an 11-year-old girl with autism, and Down syndrome. Her verbal abilities were limited, and her level of hyperactivity was high. Tia's parents knew that in order to keep Tia seated on the potty, they needed to come up with creative ideas. Tia enjoys looking at family vacation photos, and listening to classical music. Keeping Tia's preferences in mind, her parents and I created a digital album with different family vacation photos. We also placed a small CD player with classical music in the bathroom, which she could only listen to *if* she was seated on the potty. This activity was one of Tia's favorite things to do, and her parents made this activity one that she could only use in the bathroom; of course this was a highly motivating activity that Tia looked forward to. Soon, Tia was requesting to go to the bathroom, because she knew that one of her favorite activities was there. The use of a highly motivating agent provided the opportunity for frequent bathroom visits, and those visits became successful because Tia was relaxed enough doing an activity that she loved to do.

Using a tactile stimulation as a motivator: Daniel

Daniel's parents were becoming increasingly frustrated by the many unsuccessful trips to the bathroom. Daniel was keeping his pants dry for the most part, but he had learned to hold his elimination for an unbelievable amount of time; this was of concern to his parents because of the potential physical repercussions that this might have brought. In consulting with

Daniel's parents, and after a careful assessment of his baseline, as well as his likes and dislikes, we noticed that one of Daniel's favorite activities was to pull on people's fingers. Whenever anyone was in close proximity to Daniel, he would immediately begin to pull on their fingers; he would count the fingers, squeeze them, and pull them, and in doing so, Daniel would deliver to himself the sensory stimulation that he needed in stressful situations.

Daniel's parents decided to begin the potty training program with him during the Thanksgiving break. We began to put his program together in the month of October. We knew that we needed to find something that was finger-like in order to motivate Daniel. Luckily, as I was shopping at a local drug store, I ran into the Halloween display, where I found a finger-like gadget filled with a gooey substance, and I knew we had found the answer to our prayers: fingers! When our potty time arrived, we had a basket full of funny-looking squeeze balls; some were in the shape of fingers, skulls, and the like, but all of them provided the tactile stimulation that Daniel needed to relax. On the first day of potty training, Daniel experienced immediate success, and he potty trained in four days!

Tips for parents and teachers

- Your child should *only* be able to play with his or her motivators while seated on the toilet.

- Make sure you do not use any bouncy-type motivators; your child will use this as an excuse not to remain seated on the toilet.

- Your child should only be able to experience the motivators in the bathroom and absolutely in no other place but the bathroom.

- Do not use televisions as motivators; this is an activity that your child has access to in other rooms in your house and because of this, he or she will look at potty times as an option.

- Motivators should not be edible items or else they become rewards.

- Make sure that your motivators are not rewards. If you reward your child for a behavior before it is executed, then there is no reason to execute the behavior in the first place.

8. Celebrate the night before

The need to be able to predict what comes next is not a need unique to children with developmental disorders. We all need to be able to predict as many events in our days as possible, in order to help us proactively plan, and make sense of, our activities. Predictability in activities, whether leisure or otherwise, helps our children develop a mental picture of their daily activities, thereby providing the needed order to facilitate internalization of skills. Many of us like surprises, but not the type of surprises that radically change the manner in which we have been used to navigate our environment; theses types of surprises can leave us frustrated and anxious, and it is because of this, that in potty training our children with developmental disorders, we need to make sure that predictability is part of our program. The importance of providing our children with a predictable environment was discussed in previous chapters. The ability to predict what comes next helps our children organize, and discern which activities will happen in the future, thereby minimizing anxiety of performance. When our children have a sense of what will happen next, then they receive that event as a natural part of the day's activities, rather than encounter it as an unfamiliar entity, which forces them to use their defense mechanism to fight off an unfamiliar event, an event for which they have no skills.

How many times have many of us encountered unfamiliar situations that have left us frustrated because that event interfered with our plans? This is exactly what happens to our children with developmental disorders when they are unable to discern an unfamiliar situation, which leaves them losing control over what they knew before about the situation. As part of your potty training program, celebrating the event that is to come with your child offers him or her the information needed to expect a change. This approach helps them predict and plan for what is to come, and recall the skills necessary to cope with that change when needed. Celebrating the night before lets your child know what a special day is ahead, it awakens your child's expectations, creates excitement, gives your child something to look forward to, thereby decreasing his or her anxiety.

In my potty training program, we celebrated the beginning of Alex's potty training day the night before. I knew that Alex loved birthday parties so our family baked a cake decorated with a picture of a bathroom, and gift-wrapped his decorated underwear; we had birthday hats, balloons, and birthday cake. Our family had an actual "potty" party with music and all, and had Alex participate in blowing out candles and opening presents.

Our potty party gave us the opportunity to introduce potty training to Alex in a very positive manner, and the party got him excited about beginning the process of potty training. Many people wondered if Alex could even understand what we were doing, but those of us who have the privilege of parenting a child with special needs know that we take nothing for granted. My frame of mind was, and has always been, if Alex does not understand something, I will teach him; if he does understand it, he will teach me. One thing to keep in mind is to celebrate just a couple of hours before bedtime to keep your child from getting overly excited by the activity. Our potty party provided Alex with enough information about what was to come, and lowered his anxiety about the process. There are many ways to celebrate the night before your potty training program. Parents and teachers who have used Ready, Set, Potty! have been very creative about the process, and report that following this program made it easier to succeed in potty training their children with special needs. Here are just some examples of celebrating the night before potty training.

Celebrating the night before: Maria

Maria's favorite activity was bowling, so her parents designed a potty training program using bowling as a theme. The night before potty training, Maria's parents took her to the bowling alley, where they celebrated the beginning of the process as if it was a birthday party. Her family had previously mentioned to Maria that they were going to have a bowling party on Tuesday, because she was going to go pee pee in the potty. Maria was excited about going bowling, and as the days drew near, her parents kept reminding her that her potty party at the bowling alley was on Tuesday. This approach helped spark Maria's interest, awakened her expectations, and gave her something to look forward to.

Celebrating the night before: Sam

Sam's parents were very anxious about starting their potty training program because of previous unsuccessful attempts. Sam's parents decided to begin their potty training program on the Wednesday before the Thanksgiving break. In keeping with the Ready, Set, Potty! program, Sam's parents decided to celebrate the night before by having an ice cream party since this was one of Sam's favorite foods. In order for Sam's potty party to have a significant effect, his parents kept him from eating ice cream for an entire week, but made sure that the ice cream was in the freezer. Every time Sam asked for ice cream, his parents would say, "Ice cream is for potty party only." On the day of the celebration, Sam's parents talked to him about using his potty, and gave him his underwear decorated with an ice cream cone on the front of the underwear. This excited Sam, awakened his expectations, and lowered his anxiety about going to the potty.

Celebrating the night before: Mark

Animals were one of Mark's favorite things to look at. Everywhere he would go, Mark would look for pictures of animals, so his parents decided to use an animal theme for his potty training program. The night before implementing Mark's potty training program, Mark and his parents celebrated by going to a craft store that sold plastic animal figures. As part of the celebration, Mark was allowed to pick five of his favorite animal figures. Every time Mark picked an animal, his parents would say, "This is a bear, and bear goes pee pee in the potty only." This type of approach brought relevance to Mark's potty program, and helped him make a connection to what his parents expected of him. Mark's parents also observed which animals were most preferred by Mark, and used those animals to decorate his underwear, so that on the day of Mark's potty training, his parents would say, "Is your bear dry? Bear goes pee pee in the potty only." This type of approach lowered Mark's anxiety about the bathroom, and kept his attention on keeping his bear staying dry.

Tips for parents and teachers

- Do not celebrate throughout the day, as this may increase your child's anxiety.

- Make sure that your potty party theme is not over-stated, as this can produce hyperactivity in your child.

- Involve all of your family members in the process of celebrating, as well as in the potty training process.

- Celebrate about two hours before bedtime.

- Make sure that your child's gifts are the decorated underwear, and tell him or her that tomorrow he or she will go pee pee in the toilet or potty *only*.

9. Use footprints

Footprints in the Ready, Set, Potty! program are used to indicate position and encourage comfort. A comfortable and secure posture facilitates elimination. Our children are more like us than they are different. How many of us can use the bathroom with our legs crossed? Not many I hope, and if you can, you are quite creative! Our bodies need to be in a state of physical relaxation in order to respond, and the use of footprints can achieve this goal. In my particular potty training program, I noticed that sitting on the toilet seat for Alex was the thing that caused him the most anxiety, and I knew that in order to facilitate his potty training success, Alex needed to be physically relaxed while seated on the toilet.

The use of footprints helped Alex during his potty training process. To help Alex with his potty position, I drew footprints using Alex's feet as guides; I cut the footprints out, laminated them, and taped them right at the foot of the toilet. This approach gave Alex the visual directions as to where to place his feet, and helped him achieve the posture he needed to be more comfortable. If your child's feet cannot reach the floor, use a small stool and tape the footprints on it. The stool must not be removed after your child uses the potty to be used at the sink when he or she washes his or her hands; this communicates to your child that he or she can either potty or wash hands. Figure 8.2 illustrates where the footprints must be placed.

Toilet

Figure 8.2: Position of footprints

Footprints in the Ready, Set, Potty! training program are not only used to teach position and to encourage comfort. Footprints can also be used to help decrease your child's anxiety about going to the bathroom. The case studies that follow will give you some ideas as to how to use footprints as part of your potty training program.

Using footprints and help with balance: Monika

Monika's biggest potty training fear was sitting on the toilet seat. Her mom had tried everything and nothing seemed to work, it seemed like Monika was afraid of falling into the toilet. To help decrease Monika's fear and anxiety, her mom placed a set of footprints on the floor, this gave Monika the comfort she needed to relax and be able to eliminate. Monika was a non-verbal child, and was unable to voice her fear. Her small body frame made it difficult to balance while seated on the toilet, and this created a tremendous amount of anxiety over falling. Placing a step stool below the toilet did not help Monika balance, so her mother placed a chair upside down, with the legs facing Monika. Monika was able to hold on to the legs of the chair closest to her achieving the stability, security, and comfort Monika needed, while at the same time applying pressure to the bladder making it easy to eliminate.

Using colored footprints: Christian

If Christian's mother could only get him to the bathroom, he would be potty trained. Christian's challenge was not eliminating in the toilet; he would, if only his mother could get him to walk into the bathroom. To alleviate this challenge, we placed footprints from the common areas of the house leading to the bathroom for Christian to be able to focus on the footprints, rather than focus on actually walking into the bathroom. The footprints that were placed from the family room all the way to the bathroom had decorated trains of different colors. The footprints by the toilet were plain; this kept Christopher from lifting his legs while seated on the toilet to see the design. Christopher's mother kept the footprints on the floor until Christopher achieved potty training success, which only took a week.

Using colored footprints: Sara

Sara had difficulty sitting on the toilet, which of course prevented her from eliminating appropriately. Her parents placed two footprints on the floor to help Sara achieve comfort and to facilitate elimination. Sara's favorite color was red, and knowing this, her parents made sure not to use red footprints at the bottom of the toilet for Sara, as this would keep her from putting her feet on the prints as she would want to see the red footprints. Sara's parents placed a set of green footprints on the floor, and gave her one set of red footprints to hold while seated on the toilet. This approach communicated to Sara that she had to keep her feet on the green footprints, and holding the red footprints diverted Sara's attention from the fear of sitting on the toilet. Sara was successful in potty training with minimal frustration thanks to her parents' creativity in helping her become comfortable while using the toilet.

Tips for parents and teachers

- Make sure that the footprints you use are not visually distracting for your child.

- Sit on the toilet yourself, and place your child's footprints at the same distance and space that you would need to place your feet to identify an approximate comfort level for your child.

- Do not use neon colored paper to create your footprints, as neon colors are stimulating for our children.

- Do not decorate your footprints with stickers or anything else you think your child might like, as this might keep your child from using the footprints as guides.

- Make sure your footprints are the exact size of your child's feet; this will ensure that your child will step on the footprints covering the whole area, and will not distract him or her if edges of the footprints are noticeable.

10. The toilet seat

One of the greatest sources of anxiety for our children with developmental disorders is the fear of sitting on the toilet seat to eliminate. This area can create a tremendous amount of fear for our children, and seems to be an area that creates the same amount of anxiety for parents of children with developmental disorders as well. As previously discussed, minimizing our children's anxiety over potty issues is half the potty training success; the other half is in presenting our children with information that clearly defines the boundaries, expectations, and rewards of potty training. Toilet seats are uncomfortable by nature, and that is why we find items such as padded seats on the market that provide some level of comfort for people when using the restroom.

Our children are more like us than they are different, and if we keep this in mind, potty training becomes an easy skill to teach. One thing that helped my son to minimize his anxiety over potty training was consideration of his posture and comfort when using the restroom. In keeping with our theme, I placed one balloon sticker on the front lid of the toilet seat, and one on the back lid of the seat as well. This helped Alex know where he was supposed to place his bottom on the seat, while at the same time helping him catch himself eliminating. This was the beginning of establishing the critical connection between expectations, actions, and reactions. Strategically placing stickers on the toilet seat is an easy way to help your child focus on what he or she is expected to do, while at the same time providing him or her with enough visual stimulation to use as directions to execute the expected steps. Take a look at Figure 8.3 to guide you as to where to place your visuals/ stickers on the toilet seat to help your child achieve a comfortable posture. The aim of using this strategy is for your child to look at the front sticker on the seat, thereby creating the opportunity to catch themselves eliminating, and giving you the unique opportunity to assert to them what they need to do, and to reward them immediately for having done it.

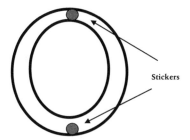

Figure 8.3: Position of stickers on the toilet seat

One of the questions that I am often asked in my potty training consultations is whether or not a toilet seat insert or a child's potty should be used during potty training. It is not recommended to use an insert or a child's potty with children with developmental disorders. The reason is that once our children have learned to problem solve, or how to balance themselves on the toilet, they expect the same feeling, or physical information, to be given to them when using other bathrooms; this can create a problem of generalization of skills. If you are not prepared to carry a toilet seat insert or a child's potty everywhere you go—which is unrealistic—then we must teach the appropriate skills all at once. Parents that have used the Ready, Set, Potty! program have become very creative about ways to help their children with special needs achieve this very important milestone, and the following case studies illustrate just how creative you too can be when implementing your individualized potty training program. Let's look at some of those creative examples.

Using pictures of roses on the toilet seat: Cristina

Not only was Cristina confused about what her parents expected of her every time they took her to the restroom, she was also terrified of sitting on the toilet; it felt uncomfortable, cold, and the fear of falling into the toilet took over her ability to successfully eliminate in the toilet. Cristina's parents had tried to potty train her on four different occasions, and met with resistance from Cristina, leading them to believe that she was not ready to be potty trained. We knew that Cristina loved pictures of red roses, so her parents placed a sticker of a yellow rose—of least interest for her—on the back part of the toilet seat, and a sticker of a red rose on the front of the toilet seat; her favorite rose color. Placing the sticker of the red rose in the middle of the front of the toilet seat encouraged Cristina to keep her legs open in an effort not to cover the red rose sticker, and decreased her anxiety since her focus was no longer on falling into the toilet, but on looking at the red colored rose sticker on the seat. Within seconds of trying this approach, Cristina successfully eliminated for the first time on the toilet, her parents immediately intervened with a positive reward, and Cristina was able to make the connection between cause and effect, which is a critical part of any successful outcome.

Help with balancing on the toilet seat: Ray

Ray's biggest challenge was not the issue of eliminating in the potty. He could do this if his parents held his arms at his sides, which provided him with balance and security. We needed to help Ray become independent in potty training, and understand that he could achieve this same balance and security without his parents. Ray was a child with significant multiple disabilities that included fine and gross motor skills issues. His small frame did not provide him with enough strength to help him achieve the balance he needed to achieve comfort while seated on the toilet. In assessing Ray's needs and fears, we decided that if Ray could access that balance himself, his potty training program would be successful regardless of his perceived limitations. Since Ray needed his arms to be held at his sides by someone while seated on the toilet, we decided to tie two regular elastic headbands to each side of the toilet. The headbands needed to be tied in a way that Ray could slide his hands through each one of them, with the headbands being tight enough to offer Ray that sensory stimulation, and the security he needed to achieve that balance. Once this approach was implemented, Ray soon began to problem solve, and achieved that balance without using his headbands.

Using a theme of bears on the toilet: Emily

Emily was a child with significant hyperactivity issues, coupled with limited communication skills. Emily's hyperactivity got in the way of her being able to sit on the toilet, getting up several times because of her lack of understanding of what was expected of her. Emily absolutely loved bears; this is the theme that her parents chose for her potty training program. Emily's parents placed two bear stickers on the toilet seat, but this did not seem to be enough for Emily to focus on the issue at hand. Emily's parents knew that if Emily was to achieve success in the area of potty training, they needed to step up her program providing her with added incentives to successfully potty train. Not only did Emily's parents use stickers on the seat, they also painted a bear inside of the actual toilet! This was creativity at its best, a clever way to help Emily focus on the bear that was *in* the water.

Emily's parents remembered that whenever Emily wanted a snack, water, or anything else, she would ask, "Bear wants juice, bear wants water…" Therefore, when Emily was taken to the rest room, her parents would say, "Bear wants potty—pee pee." This is all it took for Emily to potty train in a week, and for her to be able to willingly sit on the toilet, and even ask for the bathroom when the need arose. Was this a case of the best ideas coming from desperation? No, this was a case of best ideas being generated by creativity.

Tips for parents and teachers

- Make sure that the stickers/visuals that you place on the toilet seat are not easy to remove.

- Place your stickers/visuals right side up to keep your child from moving around or tilting his/her head to access the visual.

- Refer to the sticker/visual when your child is on the toilet, this will divert the attention from the actual task, and still keep your child relaxed enough to be able to eliminate.

- If possible, do not stand too close to your child singing, or do anything that will distract your child from the task at hand when he or she is on the toilet, this provides more anxiety to an already difficult situation for them.

- Make sure that your visuals are not overly busy, as this may over-stimulate your child, keeping him or her from focusing on the task at hand.

11. Create a behavior strip

In a previous chapter, and throughout our potty training program, we have discussed the importance of implementing a program that involves order, predictability and routine, as critical components of successful teaching, and acquisition of new skills. As part of our Ready, Set, Potty! program, the use of a behavior strip is important for our children with developmental disorders to understand the expectations of going to the bathroom in a clear and concise manner. A behavior strip visually communicates to your child *what* behaviors he or she is expected to execute. Behavior visuals provide your child with self-monitoring reminders as to *how* he or she must execute certain behaviors, and answer your child's question as to *when* to execute these behaviors. As part of our potty training program, a behavior strip must be posted preferably above the toilet tissue dispenser. The placement of a behavior strip helps children rely on what is visually available, giving them the independence they need to be successful, rather than encouraging their reliance on another human being to successfully execute a skill.

Alex needed clear directions and reminders of what was expected of him when he used the bathroom, and he needed to be independent in accessing these reminders. I provided him with a behavior strip to achieve this end. A behavior strip is a list of steps of the desired behaviors that clearly define the order in which the behaviors should be performed. I used a sequence of pictures/word visuals to indicate the desired behavior, and posted the behavior strip above the toilet tissue dispenser to the right of the toilet. This step was necessary so that even when Alex was frustrated, he could access the information he needed. Figure 8.4 is an example of Alex's behavior strip.

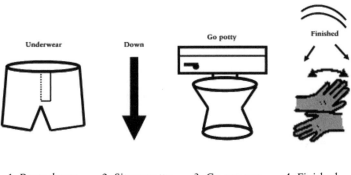

Underwear	Down	Go potty	Finished
1. Pants down	2. Sit on potty	3. Go pee pee	4. Finished

Figure 8.4: Alex's behavior strip

The use of visuals facilitates the learning of any skill for children with developmental disorders whether they are readers or not. Visuals provide reminders that help children access the needed information to execute skills across environments, and in our Ready, Set, Potty! program, visual aids speed up the rate at which potty training skills are attained.

Making the behavior strip clear: Robert

Robert knew what he needed to do once he got to the bathroom because his mother would go through the steps with him. Robert was very close to potty training, if he could only remember what to do once he was in the bathroom. In reality, Robert was not potty trained, his mother was! Without her constant input, Robert was not able to access the information he needed to become independent in the area of potty training. Robert's parents placed a behavior strip as directed, but Robert did not seem the least bit interested in following the directions.

The information as to what Robert was supposed to do was visible to every one, except to Robert. Robert's behavior strip was clouded by the many decorations that his mother placed in the bathroom so the instructions that he needed to access got lost, and in Robert's eyes, the visuals became part of the overall bathroom decor. Knowing this information, Robert's mother re-designed the behavior strip by using a different color of paper for each instruction, and by using letters on each picture, instead of numbers, since Robert's favorite activity was to sing the alphabet. Further, Robert's mother used larger pictures to develop his behavior strip making it easy for Robert to pay attention to it. Once her behavior strip was developed, Robert's mother toned down her bathroom theme decorations to ensure that the primary message of going to the bathroom would not get lost in all the visual information that Robert had when going to the bathroom. Within a few hours, Robert began to focus on the potty skills that he was required to execute, and by the end of the day, he had become independent in pulling his pants down, sitting on the potty, and eliminating! The behavior strip worked well for Robert, because his individual differences were taken into account.

Adapting the behavior strip: Lena

Lena's parents became increasingly frustrated by her refusal to pull down her pants when she went to the potty. She would let her parents know that she wanted to go to the toilet, but once in the bathroom, Lena would have accidents before sitting on the toilet. Lena's potty training program was lacking one important element: order. Lena was aware of the expectations, but was unable to access the information needed to execute what was required of her. Although Lena's parents had so far followed the Ready, Set, Potty! program, they did not feel they needed to implement visuals, since Lena was able to follow simple step directions, read simple words, and fully understood —they believed—what the expectations were.

Lena's behavior strip was not placed above the toilet tissue dispenser since she had a history of playing with toilet tissue. Her parents placed the behavior strip on a hard board, which she held when seated on the potty. One of Lena's strongest skills was the concept of finishing. It seemed that if she knew when something would be over, she would then do what was asked of her however difficult the task was. For Lena, I designed a behavior strip that had flaps at the top of the picture for her to be able to close each flap to cover each picture as she executed the skill. Lena's sense of finishing something was so strong, that she would not close the flap to a certain picture until she performed that skill. Thanks to Lena's strong sense of beginning and end, she was able to independently and successfully potty train.

Using objects in the behavior strip: Angel

Some of Angel's biggest challenges were related to his limited communication skills, and his limited ability to track and discriminate pictures or symbols. These limitations became roadblocks to his parents' ability to implement an effective potty training system, because they felt limited in their approach. Through our consultation, I knew that using objects as the primary means to relate information to Angel would be critical to his success in potty training. Angel's parents and I developed a behavior visual using miniature doll's clothes velcroed to the wall that faced the toilet. In using actual objects, Angel was able to understand what his parents expected of him when going to the bathroom.

I believe that if you are going to teach something, you should teach it well, and take advantage of the opportunity by teaching multiple skills. Not only did we post an object behavior strip, but we also attached a word and a picture to each item to begin to teach Angel to track and to discriminate pictures, knowing that this would be critical to increasing his communication skills. The visual strip worked beautifully for Angel, and along the way, he learned to discriminate and accept pictures as a mode of communication. Angel is now a young man who achieved an unbelievable amount of independence across different environments. He is one of the most proficient communicators that I have yet to meet, and he does so using a communication device that at the beginning of his training involved the use of object/pictures/words.

Tips for parents and teachers

- Do not use any of your theme-related decorations to develop your behavior strip; doing so might be too distracting for your child, and might interfere with his or her ability to follow the directions. The aim is to keep your child from placing his or her focus on the decorations, rather than on the pictures themselves.

- If your child is not responding to your behavior strip, think about using larger size pictures, different color paper, or actual photographs, this will center your child's focus.

- Make sure that your strip only involves three to four directions, and that the directions follow a simple order from left to right, or from top to bottom.

- Use the least amount of words necessary to help your child follow the instructions in the behavior strip; too many words may give your child too much auditory stimulation, which may in turn increase his or her anxiety level.

- Point to each instruction in your behavior strip, and ask your child what is next.

- From the beginning of your potty training program, use clothes that will provide your child with ease in pulling up/down. Buttons, snaps, and zippers involve the use of your child's fine motor skills that can prove frustrating. Easy access is the key to success.

12. Use a bathroom basket

If you walk into most bathrooms, what do you see? Books and magazines. Have you ever wondered why or how these items became a staple in most bathrooms? Bathrooms are *the* only rooms in our homes that have a single purpose. Most other rooms in our homes have dual purposes and can be used to relax, watch television, eat, but the bathroom... this is a room with a single purpose. That single purpose element renders bathrooms boring by most standards, hence magazines in the bathroom. Keeping in mind that our children with developmental disorders are more like us than they are different, Ready, Set, Potty! calls for the availability of items—motivators—in the bathroom to help keep your child's focus, and to help him or her remain seated on the toilet.

Placing a basket next to the toilet was a huge part of my son's potty training program. I placed a small basket next to the toilet with new books for Alex to look at when he was on the potty. These books included books of animals with as little words as possible to avoid distractions. There was also a small album with pictures of our family's last vacation, a small hand-held fan, pictures of Alex's previous birthday parties, and his potty story, which we will discuss in a later section. I found that providing Alex with a basket full of motivators enticed him to stay seated on the toilet longer than he would have agreed to otherwise. The only time Alex could play with the items in the basket was when he was seated on the toilet. Other parents that I have worked with in the past have used items such as musical toys, squeeze balls, or a glove filled with rice as sensory motivators. The use of motivating items is where accounting for your child's individual sensory needs comes in handy. Just remember one very important thing: do not allow your child to play with any of the motivators in the basket unless he or she is seated on the toilet. The items that you place in the baskets are not rewards; they are motivators, which means that your child will borrow them from the basket, and return them after he or she has used the restroom. Creativity is the name of the potty game, and as you can see in the examples that follow, many parents have become very creative in the use of motivators in the basket.

Using a bathroom basket: Pete

Pete's parents had decided to embark on the potty training journey once again, and this time were fully dedicated and committed to helping Pete achieve success. One of the first things that Pete's parents did was to evaluate Pete's likes and dislikes, and to try to incorporate items of high value to Pete into his potty training program. Pete's parents knew that Pete's motivation was low; this presented a serious challenge for them, because Pete had significant tactile sensory issues that interfered with his ability to acquire skills across different areas. In helping Pete's parents evaluate his likes and dislikes, I noticed that one of the things that Pete was highly attracted to was hair. Everywhere Pete went, he would reach to touch people's hair. Pete's parents had always viewed this as a significant behavior issue; little did they know that this same attraction was the key to helping Pete become independent in his potty training program.

When putting Pete's bathroom basket together, we decided to get three or four wigs with different hair textures. We placed those wigs in Pete's bathroom basket and offered them to him only when he was seated on the toilet. This approach yielded immediate results and within two weeks, Pete was fully potty trained. Pete understood that the only time he could touch hair was when he was seated on the toilet. The availability of the wigs in Pete's basket met his sensory needs several times a day. Not only did this approach help Pete to achieve potty training success, but his desire to touch other people's hair diminished as well!

Using a bathroom basket: Toni

Toni's parents were ready to embark on the potty training journey knowing that it would take creativity to help Toni achieve this goal. One of Toni's biggest challenges was her inability to sit in one spot for a determined amount of time; her sitting time was between 7 and 11 seconds. Her parents were aware that they needed to put together a basket full of motivators that would entice Toni to remain seated on the toilet. In keeping Toni's individual difference in mind, her parents gathered several family photos, and used these photos to create three small photo albums that Toni could look at while on the toilet. One of Toni's photo albums showed pictures of ceiling fans, which was one of her favorite items. Gathering Toni's favorite photos helped her to stay seated on the toilet, and Tony was able to go to the toilet with minimal effort.

Using a bathroom basket: Jackie

Ready, Set, Potty! This is exactly what Jackie did once her parents developed and implemented a potty program that was relevant to her. Old habits die hard only in the absence of creativity. Jackie's parents were ready to help her potty train not only because she was 20 years old, but also because Jackie's lack of potty training skills was standing in the way of her road to independence. In spite of Jackie's significant limitations, she had learned to work on assembling projects, an activity that was of high interest to her. Jackie's lack of independence in the area of potty training had prevented her from acquiring gainful employment, because her attention was centered on the activities she was involved with, and she was unable to listen to her body's need for elimination.

In developing and implementing Jackie's potty training success, we needed to use in her potty training the very thing that kept her from going to the bathroom when the need arose. Jackie's parents decided to fill her bathroom basket with an activity that required assembly. The only time Jackie was able to assemble a small bracelet—her favorite piece of jewelry—was when she was seated on the toilet. Once Jackie eliminated in the appropriate place, her instructions were to place her assembly materials back in the basket. Jackie quickly learned that if she wanted to assemble something, she needed to be on the toilet, and produce the expected results. It took Jackie a couple of weeks to understand this new concept and after the behavior became consistent, her parents began to remove the assembly items—one by one—into a workstation that was set for her in the living room. Another strategy that Jackie's parents used was to develop and implement a toilet schedule, which was placed on Jackie's workstation. Jackie's parents also used a timer set for every two hours to remind Jackie to go to the bathroom. Soon, Jackie no longer needed the assembly materials in the basket, and was successful in securing a part-time job assembling phone parts. At work, Jackie still uses a watch that is set to beep every two to three hours, she carries a small bracelet in her purse, which she takes to the bathroom with her, and which takes her no more that five minutes to assemble. When finished, Jackie dis-assembles her bracelet, places it back in her purse, and goes back to her station to work. Jackie's parents are very proud of the tremendous amount of independence Jackie has gained as a result of being potty trained.

Tips for parents and teachers

- Carefully evaluate your child's likes and dislikes, and use this information to assemble your basket.

- Take care in choosing the items for your basket. Do not use anything that will bounce, or make loud noises, as this might break your child's concentration.

- If you are a teacher, and if you do not have a bathroom in your classroom, use a small basket or a see-through bag to place your motivating items in.

- Make sure to restrict the availability of the items in your basket to bathroom times only.

- Do not, under any circumstances, use a television in the bathroom to help your child remain seated on the toilet. This type of item is one that your child has access to in other parts of your house, and because watching television is an activity that is long in terms of duration, it would be considered a reward, not a motivator.

- Use the least amount of words possible while your child is seated on the toilet to avoid over-stimulation, and a power struggle.

- Counting to 20 is a good strategy to use in helping your child eliminate; remember, the concept of finishing is of high relevance to your child.

- Do not sit your child on the toilet for longer than five minutes; more than this constitutes punishment in your child's eyes.

13. Give a reward

A reward is a powerful tool that we all use every day, and in nearly every aspect of our lives. A reward is not a bribe. A bribe is when you give something to someone expecting a desired *initial* reaction, without expecting a long-term change in behavior. For example, a parent may say, "You can watch a movie, when you pick up your toys." In this type of situation, the child looks at the reward, evaluates its worth, follows through with the expected behavior, but refuses to execute the same behavior independently, because he or she has already acquired his or her desired gain. A reward, on the other hand, is something that we pay someone with for displaying a desired behavior, with the continued expectation of the re-occurrence of that behavior even after the reward is removed. A reward is something that we all need and are motivated by. It is not always a tangible item. Often a reward comes in the form of simple recognition: praise given to a person for a desired result, *and* the expectation of a change in behavior, with the giver and the taker expecting the same result whenever the desired behavior occurs.

All of us who work in paid positions or do volunteer work expect something of value—intrinsic or extrinsic—in exchange for our efforts and results. For example, I may expect a paycheck and recognition for my efforts at work; that is my reward for working. In the latter case, my reward for volunteering is intrinsic in its form and self-gratifying in nature. In my own journey in potty training my son, I had to first recognize the power of rewards. I needed to understand that if I wanted Alex to do something, I needed to communicate to him what he was getting in exchange for his actions. Our children understand the issue of receiving something for a deed more than we can appreciate. From the time our children are born, we condition them to know that if they want a certain item, they must ask for it whether this is through using pictures, signs, or augmentative communication. I call this exchange the desire-deed-reward factor. Take a moment to ask yourself, in the toilet training process, what is in it for your child? What will he or she get for displaying the desired behavior? How strong must the reward be to elicit that behavior? These may seem like simple questions to ask, but they are in all actuality important questions to answer, if we are to design an individualized plan that caters to our children's unique selves.

I knew I needed to give Alex a reason—a reward—for successfully going to the toilet. I knew that Alex liked potato chips, so I attached a see-through jar with potato chips to the tank of the toilet using Velcro. I felt that the reward needed to be immediate and visible. Every time Alex urinated in the potty, he got three potato chips as a reward. This was the only time he was able to have potato chips during the potty training process. Some of the parents that I have worked with have also successfully used bite-sized chocolates, popcorn, and ice cream.

Food can be a strong reward for our children, but one that must be used with caution. We must remember to use food along with some intrinsic rewards such as a big "hurray" for a job well done. After Alex got his chips as extrinsic rewards, I would tickle him to the tune of his favorite song, but changed the words to "Alex gets a little tickle for going potty," as his intrinsic reward. Using this approach allowed me to give Alex extrinsic, as well as intrinsic pleasure for eliminating in the potty. It is important to point out that Alex only got potato chips and a tickle when he eliminated in the potty and in no other place.

One of the most important things to keep in mind in regard to rewards is that they must be immediate, relevant, to the point, and short-term. It is not advisable to use television as a reward, since this is the type of reward that is long in duration, and since the concept of finishing is so important to our children, terminating a program before it ends is seen by our children as punishment rather than a reward. Further, rewards must last no more than a few seconds in duration, or the issue of saturation and habituation may take over the main reason why your child got the reward in the first place.

Remember that if a child can hold on to a reward for more than 30–45 seconds, then the reward loses its power. Another thing to keep in mind in terms of rewarding your child is that the reward given to him or her should only be given when the child has displayed the desired behavior. You should not reward your child for sitting on the toilet if this is not your ultimate goal. Your ultimate goal is for your child to eliminate in the toilet, and this is the behavior that you want to reward. Take a look at some of the examples that I have seen in my years of helping parents to potty train their children.

Using numbers as a reward: Rosie

Rosie loved math. From the time she was a little baby, her parents noticed that counting soothed her in times of stress, and although her parents tried to expand Rosie's interest, Rosie always reverted to numbers. Rosie was a girl with a significant communication disorder among other disabilities, and although she could barely speak, she understood numbers more than people gave her credit for. One of the biggest challenges for Rosie's parents was that Rosie was not interested in candy at all, or anything edible for that matter. Keeping Rosie's particular interest in mind, we decided to stamp her hand with addition facts. Rosie's parents would stamp a new number every time Rosie had a success in the toilet. This encouraged Rosie to use the bathroom as often as possible to get her hand stamped with the next number, or part of the equation.

Rosie did well with her potty training because the motivation was interesting and relevant to her, and her reward involved the concept of finishing something. Linking numbers and keeping in mind the importance of the concept of finishing gave Rosie the motivation to potty train in a fun and creative way. Rosie's baseline provided average elimination times enabling her parents to isolate five times during the day when they needed to take Rosie to the restroom. Every time Rosie eliminated in the toilet, she got her hand stamped with one number or part of the equation. Seeing the equation incomplete encouraged Rosie to use the restroom, since in her mind she knew how the equation was supposed to look. Here is an example of the stamps that Rosie got when she used the toilet: 5+3=8. In this case, it took five successful toilet trips in order for Rosie to complete her equation.

Using Christmas rewards: Leon

Leon absolutely loved to look at Christmas trees. Leon's parents noticed how Leon would stare at a Christmas tree, and he enjoyed decorating it as well. Leon loved decorating Christmas trees so much, that his parents decorated, and re-decorated their Christmas tree several times during the holidays just to see Leon's enjoyment in this activity. Because Christmas trees were Leon's preferred items, we decided not to potty train him in the month of November or December, since these months provided several opportunities for Leon to be exposed to Christmas trees. I advised giving Leon a couple of months to wind down from the holidays, and we decided that the beginning of March was the perfect month to potty train Leon. As part of his potty training program, Leon's parents decorated the bathroom using Christmas as their theme, and the same theme was used to decorate his underwear as well.

Leon's parents placed a small table-top Christmas tree on the sink in the bathroom that they would be using to potty train Leon. Every time that Leon had a success in the toilet, his parents would give him a small tree decoration for him to place on the tree. Leon absolutely loved his tree, and soon began to initiate going to the restroom, and eliminating successfully, just to get the next decoration.

Using a puzzle as a reward: Alex

In my potty training program with my son, I embedded Alex's favorite character into the birthday party theme. I knew that Alex loved puzzles, and keeping this in mind, I enlarged and laminated a large picture of his favorite dinosaur to poster size. I cut the dinosaur into five pieces, and placed a piece of cardboard on the wall where Alex could Velcro each part to complete the dinosaur. Every time Alex eliminated in the toilet, he would get one piece of the puzzle as his reward. Alex knew that his dinosaur was not a dinosaur without each one of the parts, so he quickly understood that he had the control and power to complete the dinosaur, and most importantly, he knew what he needed to do to accomplish his goal. Once Alex's toilet successes became more consistent, I began to slowly fade out all my theme prompts.

Tips for parents and teachers

- Use one reward at a time; too many rewards communicates to your child that there is a choice as to when to display the desired behavior.

- Make sure that your reward is short in duration. Long-lasting rewards create an issue of habituation.

- Make sure that you reward your child immediately after eliminating in the potty; this will create a learning chain in your child's mind.

- Do not wait to reward until your child has completed washing and drying his or her hands, your child will be confused as to whether he or she is being rewarded for eliminating in the potty, or washing his or her hands.

- Make sure that your child does not have access to his or her reward except when in the restroom, and only when he or she has successfully eliminated in the toilet.

- Your reward must last no more than 30–45 seconds in order to create desirability in your child.

- Your child's rewards must have a present and continuous factor in order for your child to want more of it. This approach will create in your child the desire, and the willingness to display the behavior, in order to meet his or her own expectation.

14. Create a potty story

A potty story is a story about your child that tells him or her specifically what, how, for how long and when a specific behavior is expected of him or her. Personal stories about your child are a powerful way to shape, re-shape, and teach new skills that address specific behaviors, because these stories carefully sequence the expected behaviors, while at the same time give your child clear information about his or her reward. Skills stories are not only used for potty training purposes, but also for other behaviors such as training your child to successfully participate in community outings, and social skills training as well. I have also used these types of stories to teach restaurant skills, not to bite, not to hit, or scream, among other things. If used properly, skills stories could be one of your most powerful tools to help your child achieve success in any area of his or her life.

One of the most important things to remember about skills stories is that they must be age appropriate, relevant, and to the point. A skills story must focus on one skill at a time in order to facilitate learning. I strongly recommend that you use real photographs for your potty story. You may use other graphics but in my experience, actual photographs work better. Also placing the skills story in a small photo album, so that it looks like an actual book that is easily accessible to the child is highly recommended. Take a look at Alex's potty training story.

It is Potty Time!

Page 1: picture of Alex.

Page 2: story statement: My name is *Alex* and I am two years old.

Page 3: picture of the toilet.

Page 4: story statement: This is my *potty*, where I *pee pee*, *or poo poo*.

Page 5: picture of Alex pulling down his pants.

Page 6: story statement: *First*, I pull *down* my *pants*.

Page 7: picture of Alex sitting on the potty.

Page 8: story statement: *Next*, I *pee pee*, *or poo poo* in the *potty only*.

Page 9: picture of Alex flushing the toilet.

Page 10: story statement: *Then*, I *flush* the potty.

Page 11: picture of Alex pulling pants up.

Page 12: story statement: When I *finish*, I pull my *pants up*.

Page 13: picture of Alex washing his hands.

Page 14: story statement: I *wash* my *hands*.

Page 15: picture of Alex drying his hands.

Page 16: story statement: I *dry* my *hands* with the *towel*.

Page 17: picture of a reward.

Page 18: story statement: *First*, I *pee pee* in the *potty*. *Then* I get *potato chips*.

Page 19: picture of Alex sitting on the toilet.

Page 20: story statement: I go *pee pee*, *or poo poo* in the *potty only*.

Page 21: picture of parents and child looking happy.

Page 22: story statement: I am a big boy. *Mommy* and *daddy* are *proud* of me.

(Note: words in italics denote words that need to be highlighted in yellow.)

There are a few things to keep in mind when writing your potty story. These considerations will help you create a potty story that will be effective for your child. When you write your potty story, highlight the most important words on each page in yellow. Based on the highlighted words in your potty story, your story should sound like telegraph. Telegraphic communication is a method of communication that uses coded words (impulses) to transmit a message. It is a manner of conveying information using the least amount of words, yet selecting specific words to preserve the meaning of the message. This helps our kids focus on the most important words of the story. Your potty story should sound as follows when you read it to your child:

Alex

Potty, pee pee, or poo poo

First, down pants

Next, pee pee, or poo poo potty only

Then, flush

Finish, pants up

Wash hands

Dry hands towel

First pee pee potty, then potato chips

Pee pee, or poo poo potty only

Mommy daddy proud

The assembled potty album or potty training book should be read to your child regularly throughout the day, in order to reinforce the skills that you are trying to get your child to accomplish. I recommend that you make one potty story for home, and another one for your child's school, this will ensure that your child will be able to generalize his or her new learning from one environment to the next.

Tips for parents and teachers

- Make sure that all of your photographs are arranged in the same manner either horizontally, or vertically. Mixing the layout of the photographs may disrupt your child's ability to internally transfer the information, and may decrease his or her attention span.

- Do not arrange photographs on one single page, this may be too confusing for your child, and may communicate to him or her that there is a choice as to which skills to perform.

- Use a small inexpensive photo album placing a photograph at the top page, and writing your statement on the page that follows, this approach communicates to your child which photograph corresponds to which statement.

- Be consistent with the words that you use throughout your potty story.

- Do not use stickers throughout, or decorate every page of the album with your potty theme. Decorate the front page of the album only to minimize distractions.

- Read the potty story to your child every chance you get. This means that you will be reading the potty story to your child several times a day.

- Make sure to include your child's reward within the story. I recommend that if you are using chips as I did, put an actual picture, or the actual potato chip bag as one of the photographs, doing this will make the reward real and tangible for your child, while creating a connection between action, reaction, and reward.

15. Use a first/then chart

If I complete my work at the office, then I can call it a day and go home. The predictability of this statement communicates to anyone engaged in a project what needs to be done first, in order to be able to move towards something more pleasurable, relaxing, and desirable. So what should it be any different for our children? Potty training is probably one of the biggest milestones for us, who are involved in guiding our children through the process, but it is an even bigger milestone for our children, who are expected to execute and internalize the potty training skills we are attempting to teach. I say attempting, not as a way to minimize our involvement in the process, but because the seeming difficulty involved in potty training a child with developmental disorders falls on those of us who will be going through the process, knowing very little about how to teach potty training skills.

The process of potty training a child with a developmental disorder is a lot simpler than we think. Remember the old saying that children do not come with instructions? Guess what? Our children with special needs *do* come with instructions; we just have to learn to read them properly. In previous chapters, we established that order, predictability, and routine are the key components of a well-structured program, which is the type of program that our children with developmental disorders need in order to learn, and to internalize skills that will guide them on the road to independence. In regard to our children learning potty training skills, *if* we develop a program that is predictable, *then* our children have no other option but to succeed. The concept of "*if* this *then* that" is an important component in Ready, Set, Potty! because it communicates to the child the present expectation, and the subsequent reward for meeting that expectation. It lets the child know that if they go to the toilet, then they will get their reward. I most definitely made use of the first/then principle when I helped my son potty train, and I used it as well in other areas whether I was working on Alex's communication skills, or teaching him how to buy groceries at a supermarket. Alex is now 18 years old, and he fully understands the first/then principle without having a visual as a reminder, but when he was a small boy, the first/then chart went everywhere we went. Figure 8.5 illustrates an example of a first/then potty training chart. In this example, the child is given specific instruction as to what behavior he or she is expected to display first, and the reward they will get when they display the desired behavior.

Figure 8.5: A first/then toilet training chart

Tips for parents and teachers

- Remember to laminate your first/then chart, and use Velcro to attach your pictures.

- Attach your first/then chart where it is very visible in the bathroom that you will be using for potty training.

- Have other first/then charts throughout the house, as well as one for your child to have available at school.

- Do not use loud colors to create your first/then chart; this may be distracting to your child.

- Do not decorate your first/then chart as this may decrease your child's attention span.

- In the area of "then", you may tape the actual item that your child will be rewarded with; this makes it more real, and relevant to what you are asking your child to do.

16. Bowel movements

The elimination of bowel movements during the potty training process is an area that causes parents a tremendous amount of anxiety. The tendency is for our children with developmental disorders to hold their bowel movements for a number of days. For most parents, the fear is that their children will develop extreme constipation, which could lead to medical issues, and this is why it is advisable that if your child has a history of constipation, you consult a doctor prior to beginning any potty training program. It is common for our children to hold their bowel movements for days, if not a week or so, during the process of potty training, but if your child has been medically cleared to begin a potty training system, this challenge should be viewed as positive rather than negative.

Two key issues in regard to our children holding their bowel movements should be considered. First, the holding of bowel movements should be viewed as positive, because it communicates to you that your child has learned to control his or her bladder or bowel, and this is a must, in order to be fully potty trained. Second, your child needs to feel that he or she has control of a scenario in which he or she has had control for the past several years; when our children realize that his or her control has been tampered with, the control issue takes over in order to compensate for a loss; this is a common human response. Having said this, let us move on to what we can do to help our children in a positive manner through resolving their bowel movement challenges.

Bowel movement elimination seems to be one of the biggest challenges for parents of children with developmental disorders during the potty training process. Do not be surprised if your child holds his or her bowel movements for a couple of days. This is a common response and one to be expected. In order to help you and your child be successful with bowel movements, Ready, Set, Potty! recommends writing a behavior strip that indicates the expected behavior, and a potty story that clearly defines those expectations just as was previously discussed. Many parents who are attempting to potty train their children for bowel movements think that since their children are already successful in urine elimination, following the entire potty training program from beginning to end is not necessary. You must remember that potty training is a chain with links, and each link is essential for the chain to be defined as a chain. If your child is already trained for what many of us call number one, you still have to follow all the steps in Ready, Set, Potty! to help your child achieve success in potty training for bowel movements as well. Remember, the reason why your child is not potty trained in bowel movement elimination is because the chain is missing a link: an important link that tells us what specific information the broken potty chain is missing. Let's look at some examples of how to help your child achieve bowel movement elimination.

Achieving bowel movement elimination: Raison

Raison was an 11-year-old boy, who was already successful in urinating in the toilet, but refused to go to the bathroom for bowel movements. His parents' biggest concern was that Raison was holding his bowel movements for five to seven days at a time. In order to help Raison understand what was expected of him, his parents developed a bowel movement story to decrease his anxiety over bowel elimination. To tackle this challenge, Raison's parents wrote a potty story similar to the one we previously discussed in this book. Raison's parents followed all the steps in the Ready, Set, Potty! program from developing a baseline to be able to predict the average times when Raison was more likely to eliminate, to decorating the bathroom underwear, using motivators, a potty story, and most importantly, they knew that Raison's reward had to be stronger than the one they used for urine elimination, in order to encourage him to use the bathroom for his bowel movements.

With his parents approaching the bowel movement challenge in a systematic manner, Raison was able to complete his bowel movement elimination training in 36 hours, and he did this with enthusiasm and no anxiety. Using a highly structured approach to potty training worked well for Raison, because his parents took into consideration his individual differences, and because they designed a well-structured program based on order, predictability, and routine.

Achieving bowel movement elimination: Juanita

One of Juanita's biggest challenges was in the area of bowel movements. Juanita was a nine-year-old girl with multiple disabilities, and a significant communication disorder. One of Juanita's biggest attributes was her ability to understand pictures, as well as her ability to process information through pictures to make sense of her environment. Juanita's strategy was to hold her bowel movements for two weeks at a time, causing her severe constipation, and physical discomfort, which resulted in severe behavior problems. To remedy the situation, Juanita's parents resorted to giving her an enema once a week to help her eliminate. Juanita's system had already become used to eliminating by using an enema only, and her body did not seem to respond to any other attempts used by her parents. In Juanita's case, her parents wrote a potty story that clearly defined the expectations using pictures of her favorite people in the family using the restroom. The pictures in Juanita's potty story were quite graphic in that they involved a picture of the product inside the toilet to help Juanita process what she needed to deposit there. It took Juanita one day to understand the expectations, and from that point forward, she no longer needed the enemas to be able to eliminate.

Achieving bowel movement elimination: Maggie

Not only did Maggie have a problem with depositing her bowel movements in the potty, but also her parents had a problem with her smearing the faeces on the wall. Every time Maggie would want to use the bathroom for a bowel movement, she would hide behind a couch and squat to eliminate, then she would smear the product all over the walls. Maggie's parents were pretty frustrated by her inability to understand the inappropriateness of her behavior, and would resort to using diapers for bowel movements only. Maggie had learned that eliminating in her underwear was not appropriate so she would get rid of the product—so she thought—by smearing it all over the walls. This was a perfect example of "out of sight out of mind." Maggie had replaced one behavior with another; this was the ultimate example of a child using problem solving skills. To help Maggie understand what behavior was expected of her in regard to bowel movements, her parents had to re-trace the steps of their potty training program. The re-tracing of their potty training program yielded a re-evaluation of Maggie's individual differences, and led her parents to institute new rewards, and motivators, along with writing a potty story, which involved the couch as not an appropriate place to eliminate. They were encouraged to move the couch to another part of the house when Maggie was not watching, in order to institute the element of surprise, and to limit Maggie's choices. In the place of the couch, they placed a planter that Maggie was not familiar with, and in the absence of resorting to something familiar when she wanted to have a bowel movement, Maggie resorted to using the potty as her only choice. Of course, her rewards and motivators were raised to a higher level to give Maggie a reason to perform the expected behavior, and to continue to make her feel as though she still had some control over her bodily functions. Needless to say, the success was immediate.

Tips for parents and teachers

- Never teach a boy to urinate standing up. Standing up for urinating gives the body a different feeling than when that child's body calls for a bowel movement. Boys who are taught to stand up to urinate usually experience more problems, and significant constipation issues.

- If your child is already trained to urinate in the toilet appropriately, but has issues with his or her bowel movements, begin the potty training process with a different theme, rewards, motivators, and potty story to avoid the issue of habituation.

- Your child's rewards must not only be different, but also significant enough to encourage your child to display the desired behavior.

- Move a couch, a planter, or any other piece of furniture to the space where your child has chosen to hide every time he or she wants to eliminate. Remember that familiarity brings comfort, and although you do not want to make your child's potty training experience an uncomfortable one for your child, you do not want to encourage comfort in inappropriate places.

- Note that not all children will have a problem with bowel movements; most children will train for both types of elimination at the same time, but in case bowel movements present a challenge for your child, remember that you have the answer to that challenge: order, predictability, and routine.

- The issue of wiping must be taught as a separate skill, in order for our children not to view wiping as an alternative to eliminating. Teach the skill of wiping hand-over-hand by placing your hand first, then your child's hand on top of yours, with a piece of toilet tissue underneath, then a wet-wipe. It is important that you make immediate contact, not a sweeping motion. Using a sweeping up and down motion on the area that needs to be wiped gives the child conflicting information as to what specific areas of their bottom to wipe, since the sweeping up and down motion touches different parts of their bodies. On the other hand, immediate contact with the part of the body that needs to be wiped gives children immediate information as to what they are expected to do. Every time your child uses the potty, help him or her wipe as directed and then say, "Your turn, you wipe."

17. Night training

Night training will happen naturally, as your child learns to control his or her body during regular potty training hours.

Most parents find that the issue of night training is not a challenging one when using a well-structured potty training program. It is important that your child wear pull-up type underwear at the beginning of night training, and only at night. You will notice that your child will stay dry for longer periods of time during the night as he or she begins the natural process of controlling his or her elimination process. Night training is one of the simplest steps in the Ready, Set, Potty! program. It usually takes the writing of a night potty story to help your child get up to use the restroom at night. A critical part of the night training process involves limiting your child's liquid intake at least 45 minutes prior to bedtime. Some valuable tips will be given to you in this section to ensure that once you wake up your child for the last potty call, he or she does not remain awake. Figure 8.6 illustrates an example of a small potty story that I used for Alex for night-time training.

Night-time   Bed

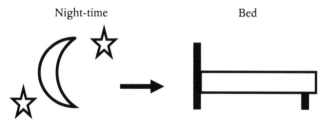

At night, I go to sleep in my bed. Sometimes when I am asleep, I want to go pee pee, I go pee pee in the toilet.

Sleep   Go to the toilet

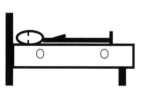 

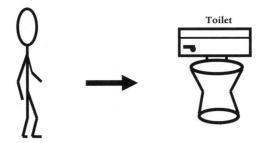

I go to the bathroom, I pee pee in the bathroom.

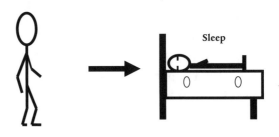

Then, I go back to sleep again.

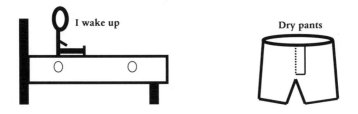

In the morning, I wake up and my pants are dry.

My mommy and daddy are proud of me.

Figure 8.6: An example of a potty story used for night-time training

One of the most common questions that I am asked through my workshop presentations is when and how to begin night-time potty training, and the difficulty involved in the process. Because of the minimal difficulty in potty training for night-time, it is recommended that this skill not be addressed until your child is successful and independent in eliminating during the day. Potty training for night-time should be addressed once the child is independent in eliminating in the potty during the daytime for a period of one to two months depending on the child. Once your child is potty trained during the day, begin night-time potty training by following the recommended steps for night-time training. As always, remember to keep your child's individual likes and dislikes in mind, and to change the type of reinforcer you used to potty train during the day. The examples that follow will give you an idea as to different strategies that I have used in night-time potty training for children with special needs.

Night training: Veronica

Veronica's parents had helped Veronica achieve an important milestone for her: potty training. Veronica was now potty trained during the day, but the issue of bedwetting became a challenge for her parents. In assessing Veronica's situation, I noticed that right before bed, her parents would give her very specific instructions to remain in her bed, and not to get up. Veronica was an eight-year-old child who was considered non-verbal, and whose parents did not realize just how much she was able to understand and process information. One of Veronica's night-time bed rituals was to drink some apple juice, and all the while, her parents kept telling her that it was bedtime, and not to get out of bed. As instructed, Veronica followed her parents' instructions and in her understanding, getting out of bed to go to the bathroom was not an option. I always caution parents to be careful of what we ask our children with special needs to do, because they will literally do it!

One of the first steps that Veronica's parents took was to change her drinking habits from juice to water, and only 45 minutes before bedtime. They then wrote a night-time potty story to give Veronica options as to what she should do when she wanted to go to the restroom and what she should do after using the restroom.

This simple step helped Veronica to potty train at night, and alleviated her parents' frustration. It took Veronica two weeks to fully understand this concept, but she understood it well, and has not wet the bed in a couple of years. The issue of going to the bathroom at night was not the challenge for Veronica; her biggest challenge was to understand that she could no longer have apple juice in bed, and this is the reason why it took Veronica two weeks to internalize this new routine.

Night training: Doug

Doug's night bedwetting turned into a nightmare for his parents, not only because when Doug wet his bed, his mother had to wake up to change the bed sheets, but also because Doug was 15 years old, and would refuse to go to sleep after wetting the bed. Doug's parents were concerned that Doug was developing a pattern that interrupted his sleep, and this issue caused great anxiety for his parents. One of the first things that Doug's parents had to understand was that Doug was indeed developing a pattern, but that he also had limited understanding of their expectations for night-time elimination. Doug was very clear as to what to do during the daytime, but night-time was another story. Doug's parents developed a potty story that not only specified the desired behavior, but also visually communicated their expectations and goals for Doug. Doug's potty story involved a picture of a dry bed, which was the desired behavior, and a staged picture of the bed with a urine stain, which was produced by using apple juice to state the undesirable behavior. Within a couple of days Doug was able to understand what was expected of him at night, and was successful in keeping his underwear dry during the night-time.

Night training: Doris

Doris' parents had to take a very different approach in potty training her for night-time. Doris would verbally repeat the steps to going to the restroom at night, but failed to do so once she was asleep. Her parents knew that one of Doris' favorite things was to receive presents, so they decided to develop a night-time potty story that clearly stated the expected behavior. Her parents developed a story that communicated to Doris what she would get in the morning *if* her pants were dry. This first/then approach was one that Doris fully understood, and as a result, night-time training was no longer a challenge for her parents. Another strategy that Doris' parents implemented was the use of a small bag decorated in Doris' favorite color, which was pink. In the bag, they put inexpensive trinkets wrapped as presents for Doris to get in the morning if, and only if, her pants and bed were dry. Doris soon began to problem solve by taking her panties off when she wanted to urinate; she would then urinate on the bed, and put her panties back on. When Doris' parents realized what she was doing, they decided to write into the potty story that she needed to keep her panties on and her bed dry in order to get a reward in the morning, and that she needed to eliminate in the toilet. Another important step that Doris' mother took was to remove all the underwear from Doris' bedroom to limit her access to them, and to keep her from using her wonderful problem solving skills. Wrapping the small trinkets as gifts was a creative approach, because Doris never knew what she was going to get whenever she reached into her surprise bag. The element of surprise encouraged Doris to succeed in her night-time training because Doris was a child who understood delayed gratification. Doris' parents also gained the confidence they needed to introduce Doris to the road to independence as a result of her success.

Tips for parents and teachers

- Limit your child's fluid intake to 45 minutes before bedtime.

- Do not offer your child apple juice or sodas two hours before bedtime, as these types of drinks change your child's elimination times by making your child eliminate more often than usual.

- At night, take your child to the bathroom 45 minutes before bedtime; take him or her again when you put him or her in bed. Do another toilet run before you go to bed, and another one before your spouse, or the last person in the house goes to bed.

- To make sure that your child goes to sleep after potty trips at night, put a dark blue light in his or her bedroom, and one in the bathroom. Also, wake your child up using the least amount of words, and speak softly to make sure that his or her brain does not alert to the full waking stage.

- Re-arrange your child's bedroom to institute the element of surprise. The concept of familiarity communicates to our children that the behaviors that they display in certain environments are the behaviors that are expected of them regardless of circumstances. When we introduce a change of environment in a positive manner, and introduce new expectations, our children's focus becomes more centered around the new environment and the new expectations within that environment in an effort to discern new skills to problem solve within the new environment. It relates to the concept of "out with the old, and in with the new."

- Do not decorate his or her bathroom.

- Remove toys, books, and any other item that could become an alternative to going back to bed for your child.

- Play soft classical music in your child's bedroom to create a relaxed atmosphere.

- Reward your child in the morning for the desired behavior, and above all, expect some accidents to happen but do not settle for this type of behavior.

Ready, Set, Potty! checklist

You are now ready to begin your potty training plan. Remember that strategically planning your potty training approach will help guide your child to potty training success.

The most important thing to keep in mind is that when you have a plan of action, there can be no other option but to succeed. Use this checklist to plan your program, and get yourself Ready, Set, Potty! and your child on his or her road to independence!

1. Meet with your child's teacher and other family members, caregivers, friends, and anyone who will be involved in your child's potty training program. Present your program to them, keeping in mind the importance of order, predictability, and routine.

2. Besides family members, think of other people that have daily/constant contact with your child:

   (1)_____

   (2)_____

   (3)_____

3. Name five people who will be involved in your potty training program:

   (1)_____

   (2)_____

   (3)_____

   (4)_____

   (5)_____

   Ready ☐

4. Pick a target day: see pp.49–53.

   Day: _____

   Why did you pick this day?_____

   Ready ☐

5. Establish a baseline. Use Table 8.2 on p.58 to monitor your child's usual elimination times.

   Ready ☐

   Give copies to: _____

   _____

   _____

6. Pick a theme: see pp.59–61.

   Theme: _____

   Necessary objects/decorations: _____

   _____

   _____

   Ready ☐

7. Decorate the bathroom and bathroom door: see pp.61–64.

   Images/pictures: _____

   Ready ☐

8. Make diapers a thing of the past: see pp.65–68.

   Strategy: _____

   Ready ☐

9. Decorate your child's underwear: see pp.68–72.

   Chosen image/decoration: _____

   Ready ☐

10. List your child's favorite motivators: see pp.73–76.

    Motivators: _____

    Number of motivators: _____

    Ready ☐

11. Celebrate the night before: see pp.77–80.

Event: _____

Guests: _____

Food: _____

Anything else required: _____

Ready ☐

12. Use footprints: see pp.80–83.

Colors: _____

Position: _____

Ready ☐

13. The toilet seat: see pp.84–87.

Image/stickers: _____

Position: _____

Ready ☐

14. Create a behavior strip: see pp.88–91.

Description/types of pictures I will use: _____

_____

_____

Placement: _____

Ready ☐

15. Use a bathroom basket: see pp.92–96.

Contents: _____

Ready ☐

16. Give a reward: see pp.96–101.

    Item: _____

    Number of rewards: _____

    When to give: _____

    Ready ☐

17. Create a potty story: see pp.101–104.

    Photographs taken of: _____

    Duplicate for school: _____

    Ready ☐

18. Use a first/then chart: see pp.105–107.

    Images/pictures: _____

    Duplicate for school: _____

    Ready ☐

19. Bowel movements: see pp.108–111.

    Different rewards: _____

    Number of rewards: _____

    When to give: _____

    Ready ☐

20. Night training: see pp.112–117.

    Different rewards: _____

    When to give: _____

    Ready ☐

CHAPTER

RECAP

Putting it all together

Congratulations, you have just achieved one of the most important milestones for your child: potty training! You can begin to enjoy your child's entrance into independence, and look forward to a lifetime of successes. Potty training is not an easy challenge for parents and teachers of children with developmental disorders, and it is not an easy skill for our children to learn and internalize as well, but designing and implementing a well-structured potty training program will facilitate an otherwise difficult process. As a parent and/ or teacher of a child with developmental disorders, you must remember that in potty training our children, we are attempting to change a behavior that has been instilled in them: one that has been part of their lives for years. Potty training a child with developmental disorders is a time of new learning, new expectations, and achievements. Because this can be a time of anxiety for our children and frustrating for parents and teachers, we must approach the issue of potty training armed with vast knowledge of how to help our children achieve success in this area.

Keeping your child's individual differences under consideration requires us, as parents and teachers, to gain knowledge of our children's unique styles of learning, their unique manner in which they process information, and their likes and dislikes, in order to design an individualized program that will lead our child to independence in potty training, and ultimately to success. One of the most important aspects of a potty training program is to ensure that the program you use is one that has as its core foundation order, predictability, and routine. These components must exist in order to achieve success; without these components, children with developmental disorders are limited in their ability to properly process information given to them.

Parents and teachers must consider the when, why, and how long issues of potty training, in order to arm themselves with confidence and power, to produce the desired behavior in their children regardless of what skills they want to teach them. It is not until we can answer these questions that we can begin to gain important information as to when we can begin a successful potty training program, why we should begin that program, and how we can go about developing an individualized potty training program for our children. Answering the when, why, and how long questions will most importantly lead you to design a specific goal with objectives giving yourself a time line to help your child acquire this very important milestone. Remember that a plan without a goal is just a wish, and a wish is just an unrealized dream.

It is also critical to understand and accept that our children are more like us than they are different. Our children with developmental disorders have the same needs as all of us have as humans. We all have the need to be nurtured, loved, and protected. Our children, much like us, have the need to understand the world around them and, just like us, they need order, predictability, and routine, in order to achieve their goals. A successful potty training program is not complete without the delineation of specific steps to achieve your goal, and planning the steps in the Ready, Set, Potty! program facilitates and shortens the process of potty training your child whether he or she has special needs or not.

How valuable is a potty training program which does not give parents and teachers tools to help their children achieve independence? A potty training program without strategies is of very little value to parents, teachers, and to our children as well. Independence in potty training, and in any other area for that matter, is only achieved when parents and teachers gain information as to how to design an individual potty training program; remember, information is power. Once you have gained the power through the information you gathered, you can begin to embark on this very important journey: potty training your child. Welcome to the road to independence; welcome to the potty training journey!

CHAPTER 10

FOLLOWING THE SEQUENCE OF THE POTTY TRAINING STEPS

Ready, Set, Potty! sequence and steps

For your potty training to be successful, it is critical that all the steps in the Ready, Set, Potty! program be followed sequentially and simultaneously, even if your child is already trained for urinating. Remember that potty training is a learning chain of events that must be internalized, in order for our children with developmental disorders to be successful in the acquisition of potty training skills. The internalization of skills will enable your child to generalize his or her new learning from one environment to the next. Let's summarize the steps in the Ready, Set, Potty! program.

Steps to potty training

1. *Pick a target day.* Pick the day you want to start your potty training program. November and December— winter—are the best times to potty train. These are the months when our bodies retain less liquid, and our elimination times become more consistent.

2. *Establish a baseline.* Develop a baseline of your child's elimination times. A baseline is important to determine your child's potty pattern. Share this information with your child's school as well, to ensure generalization of skills.

3. *Pick a theme.* Picking a potty theme will give your child a valid reason for potty training, it will help to decrease anxiety, and it will make the potty training program relevant to your child.

4. *Decorate the bathroom and bathroom door.* Use your theme to decorate the bathroom, making sure the bathroom is decorated when your child is not looking. The element of surprise helps minimize anxiety.

5. *Make diapers a thing of the past.* Use regular white, cotton underwear for boys, nylon panties for girls. Use pull-ups during night-time only.

6. *Decorate your child's underwear.* Decorate the underwear according to your potty theme. This helps your child listen to his or her body needs for elimination.

7. *List your child's favorite motivators.* It is important to remember that motivators are items to encourage your child to perform a task. These motivators differ from rewards in that motivators are items that you child will borrow while seated on the potty, while rewards are items that your child keeps. Use motivators that appeal to your child's senses in the following areas:

   • visual sense

   • olfactory sense

   • gustatory sense

   • tactile sense

   • auditory sense.

8. *Celebrate the night before.* This will let your child know that a special day is ahead, it will awaken his or her expectations, and create excitement. You can give the new underwear as a gift.

9. *Use footprints.* Place footprints on the floor by the toilet. Footprints are used to indicate position and encourage comfort. Tape the footprints where your child can see them, and at the point where he or she can place their feet on them, and/or use them as reminder tracks leading to the restroom. Train both girls and boys to sit for urination.

10. *The toilet seat.* Place a sticker on the back and front of the toilet lid to direct you child as to where to place his or her bottom. Use a stepstool if needed. A "dog bone" pillow can be placed between the child's legs and stomach to allow him or her to lean forward, or you can use a vibrating pillow to stimulate the bladder. Note: do not use toilet inserts.

11. *Create a behavior strip.* A behavior strip is used to visually sequence your child's behavior while on the toilet. Place the behavior strip right above the toilet tissue dispenser.

12. *Use a bathroom basket.* Place a basket next to the toilet. This basket should contain surprises such as books, music and toys; these are your child's motivators, *not* his or her rewards.

13. *Give a reward.* The chosen reward *must* be immediate and temporary; delayed rewards are not recommended for daytime potty training. Rewards are important to motivate the child to display the desired behavior. Rewards can be extrinsic/intrinsic. Velcro a transparent container on top of the toilet with the reward in it; it must be visual to the child.

14. *Create a potty story.* A potty story is a pictorial story about your child. This story must be sequential and relevant. Remember to:
    - consider your child's likes and dislikes
    - choose a strong reinforcer
    - make your potty story relevant
    - clearly define the expected behavior
    - carefully sequence target behavior
    - make it fun and simple
    - highlight the key words in the story with a yellow marker.

15. *Use a first/then chart.* Use the first/then chart to help your child understand what is expected of him or her, and what they will receive in exchange for displaying the desired behavior.

16. *Bowel movements.* Increase the level and value of your bowel movement reward, and write a potty story to specify the desired behavior.

17. *Night training.* Do not get frustrated about potty training your child for night training; this issue is usually taken care of when your child has learned to control his or her eliminations during the day, but if night potty training presents a challenge for you and your child, use a night-time potty story to address this issue.

You are now ready to develop and implement your potty training program. You may find it helpful to use the checklist on pp.118–122. It will take about a week or so to develop an individualized program for your child and then to gather and prepare all the equipment that you need. I recommend to parents and teachers that they put the program together all at once, since this is the type of toilet training program that must be followed sequentially, and simultaneously—no one step is done in isolation. Make sure that when you are ready to implement your program, you do so following all the steps in the potty training sequence. Ready, Set, Potty! is designed to help parents and teachers of children with developmental disorders implement a well-structured program that facilitates and shortens the length of potty training. Order, predictability, and routine are key components to successful teaching, and implementing a program that involves these components provides a clear direction not only to parents and teachers of children with developmental disorders, but also to the wonderful children that you will be teaching these skills to. Welcome aboard, and let's get Ready, Set, Potty!

CHAPTER 11

TIPS FOR PARENTS AND TEACHERS

- *Schedule.* A visual schedule can be incorporated to help your child establish a potty routine, and to keep the person who is helping in the potty training process accountable.

- *Visual cues.* Use a picture of the bathroom, or a magnet in the form of a toilet to help your child verbalize his or her needs. Show your child these items every time you take him or her to the bathroom.

- *Verbalizing.* Use the same words consistently. In addition, use, "The rule is…" Children with developmental disorders understand this concept.

- *Language.* Change your language from "Let's go potty" to "*You* need to go potty."

- *Night training.* This usually takes care of itself once day training is completed; this is an issue that should not be addressed until your child is independent in eliminating during the daytime.

- *Bowel movements.* Do not worry about the issue of bowel movements until your child is independent in urinating during the daytime. Nevertheless, encourage it on every potty trip.

- *Generalization.* Begin taking your child to different bathrooms around the house, and out in the community. Make special trips to the store just to go to the toilet.

Remember to try using different bathrooms within your home only when your child is well on his or her way to potty independence.

- *Support system.* Enlist the help of others whenever necessary.

- *Attitude.* Confront the challenge of potty training your child expecting success; failure is not an option in training our children to acquire skills that will lead to independence.

- *Girl or boy.* Teach a male child to sit down to urinate in order to avoid future problems with bowel movements.

- *Element of surprise.* If your child has found a preferred place to eliminate other than the bathroom, re-arrange the furniture in that place to offer your child no other option but to eliminate in the potty.

- *Rewards.* Use only one reward at a time to make sure that you do not run out of options if you should need to re-vamp your program.

- *Day to begin.* Begin potty training on a Wednesday, or a Thursday, in order to ensure that your child will be exposed to the same approach both at home and at school; this will help you tackle the issue of regression.

- *Checklist.* Use the checklist on pp.118–121 to check your steps to make sure that you have not skipped any of them.

- *Celebrate.* Give your child credit when he or she experiences success however small the success might be. Remember that small steps lead to greater things.

- *Your role.* Remember that you are your child's coach; potty training is not a forced skill; rather, it is a learned skill, and you are there to support your child in his/her attempts.

- *Time.* Sit your child on the toilet for no more than three to five minutes, any more than that may be viewed by him or her as punishment.

- *One at a time.* Do not potty train multiple children at the same time. Choose to potty train the child with the most challenges first. More often than not, the others will follow.

- *Difficulty in eliminating.* For children who have difficulty eliminating, I recommend the use of a small long pillow, or vibrating pillow between their legs and abdomen to stimulate the bladder.

- *Re-evaluate.* If after a week of potty training you do not see *any* change however small it may be, do not change your potty training program, this will only confuse your child. Rather, re-evaluate your approach and ask yourself if your existing program is one that is heavily rooted in order, predictability, and routine. Re-visit your potty approach, and know that your child is doing what he or she has been trained to do. Now ask yourself if you are doing what you are supposed to do.

- *Distance.* Do not stand too close to your child, sing songs, or read books to him or her during potty times. Remember a very important concept: do as much as you can to teach your child new skills, but as little as possible to encourage independence.

- *Consistency.* Be consistent and predictable with your potty training program.

- *Accidents.* View potty accidents as opportunities to get closer to your goal.

- *Do not give up.* The more times you try and then stop the potty training process, the more difficult the process becomes.

- *Involve others.* If you get frustrated, have a friend or family member look for inconsistencies in your approach, and have them step in to change the rhythm of the potty training process.

- *When changing an accident.* When your child has a potty accident, take him or her to the bathroom and change them standing up. Lying your child on the floor to change an accident communicates to him or her that the environment has not really changed a whole lot from when he or she used diapers.

- *Changing clothes.* Keep a number of changing clothes handy in the bathroom to change your child in case there is an accident.

- *Enjoy.* Embrace this wonderful time of transition and growth with your child.

- Most importantly—*have fun!* This *will* be the last toilet training program you will need!

CHAPTER

FREQUENTLY ASKED QUESTIONS

The main problem with beginning any potty training program lies in the issue of unanswered questions: questions that without answers only set us up for disappointment in the process of potty training. I find that just as our children with developmental disorders need to know why, when, and how, so do we need to know this, in order to have a clear plan of action to help our children become successful with their potty training skills, or any other skill for that matter. When my son got his diagnosis of severe autism at the age of two, I was already in the field of special education, nevertheless, this in no way helped me to deal with the diagnosis, much less the immediate challenges that accompanied our diagnosis. I knew what I needed to do, but the grieving process and the unanswered questions temporarily paralyzed me to the point of fear. After my initial reaction, I knew that one of the main issues that I needed to address was the issue of potty training Alex if I wanted him to become independent. I consulted with many potty training experts only to be told that I just had to sit him on the toilet and wait until he eliminated. Well, this of course did not work, and my frustration level with my perceived inability to potty train my son mounted to learned helplessness.

I strongly believe that the most brilliant ideas come out of parental frustration, so I decided to develop and implement a potty training system that was based on order, predictability, and routine: a system that communicated to my son my expectations, and one that was visual in nature, and fun for both Alex and me, hence Ready, Set, Potty! Alex potty trained in three days, and I knew thereafter that only success would await us in our road to Alex's independence. Alex is now 18 years old, and his disability is no longer considered severe; Alex is at the high-moderate level, and continues his road to independence experiencing success at every turn. This year, Alex has accomplished yet another important milestone: gainful employment. I, like you, had several questions regarding potty training my son, and answering those questions helped relieve the anxiety and frustration that I experienced at the time. I have been teaching parents, therapists, teachers, and caregivers of children with special needs individualized training strategies, as well as potty training skills, worldwide, and am proud of the many children that have acquired independence skills across different areas. To the many children that I have helped potty train, I say: keep on trying to be all that you were designed to be. To parents and caregivers of children with special needs, I say: never, ever give up, the journey has just begun. I want to share with you some commonly asked questions that present frustration for parents and teachers of children with special needs. I know that these answers will help you in designing your potty training program.

Question 1: When should I start potty training my child with special needs?

Answer: As previously discussed, your child is ready to potty train at about three years of age regardless of disability, or perceived limitations.

Question 2: Can I potty train a child who is non-verbal?

Answer: Absolutely! Your child's verbal skills need not to be present in order for him or her to achieve independence in potty training. All children can communicate whether this is verbally, through signs, pictures, or behavior. You just have to be aware of what mode or behavior your child uses to communicate his needs and wants.

Question 3: Is it possible to potty train children whose special needs are severe, or a child with multiple disabilities?

Answer: Your child's disabilities should never be a roadblock for him or her to learn new skills. The difference in potty training a child with significant disabilities lies in the manner in which you would arrange and present a potty training program to him or her.

Question 4: Does Ready, Set, Potty! work primarily for children with autism?

Answer: Ready, Set, Potty! is a potty training program for children of all abilities and disabilities. Children with significant disabilities will take longer to potty train, on average about two weeks longer, but a well-structured, well-designed program will help any child achieve potty training success.

Question 5: What if my child does not respond to the Ready, Set, Potty! program?

Answer: If after a week you notice no change in behavior, however small, you must not change your program; rather, change your approach, and you will experience success.

Question 6: What if this program does not work for my child?

Answer: Failure should never be part of the equation in helping our children acquire independence skills. View so-called failures as opportunities to re-evaluate the manner in which you present information to your child, and tell yourself that you and your child can, and will, succeed in this and any other skill that you want your child to achieve.

Question 7: I just had another baby; should I attempt to potty train my first child, who has special needs, now?

Answer: The birth of another child is a significant change for both parents and children. Wait until your newborn is about six months, and your child with special needs has become used to the baby's presence before you introduce your child with special needs to another significant change.

Question 8: Who should be involved in the potty training process?

Answer: The active involvement of parents, teachers, and other caregivers involved in a child's life is important in order for our children with special needs to fully internalize and generalize the skills that you are trying to teach him or her, and to provide you, as his or her parents the needed support to minimize your own frustrations.

Question 9: My child is close to potty training, do I have to follow all the steps in sequence in Ready, Set, Potty!?

Answer: Yes, all the steps in Ready, Set, Potty! must be followed sequentially, and simultaneously, in order to achieve success. Think of potty training as a chain. Every chain becomes a chain because of individual links, and links are important because without them, a chain is not a chain. When a chain is broken, it is most likely because one of the links has disconnected, or because one of the links has broken. A broken link disconnects the chain from the rest of the links, and the information needed to be a complete chain is not present; that chain ceases to be a chain.

Question 10: What if my child cries, and refuses to follow the potty training program?

Answer: This is what is called the battle of the wills, and through this battle, your child tries to hold on to an area in which he or she has had control. The battle of the wills is a real concept in any potty training program, and this is where individualizing your child's potty training program by making it fun and relevant will help.

Question 11: My child has medical problems related to elimination, should I start any potty training program anyway?

Answer: If your child has medical issues, never start a potty training program without consulting your doctor. If your child's doctor agrees that this is a good time to begin your potty training program, then you have been given the green light to begin.

Question 12: How long should I make my child sit on the potty?

Answer: Your child should only sit on the potty for three to five minutes at a time. Any more than that becomes punishment for him or her, and will shed a negative light on potty training. The aim is to keep our potty training positive.

Question 13: Can I use training underwear during potty training?

Answer: No. Training pants provide the same feeling as diapers. Because training pants are so close to the body, when a child has an accident, training pants provide that feeling of comfort that you want to discourage.

Question 14: Should I read a book to my child, or sing a song to him or her while seated on the toilet?

Answer: Absolutely not. Our aim in potty training is to help our children rely on themselves to execute skills. Being close to your child while he or she is seated on the toilet is distracting, and encourages him or her to see you as a must-have facilitator to execute that task.

Question 15: My child has significant food allergies, must I use foods that he or she is allergic to in order to have success using Ready, Set, Potty!?

Answer: Food allergies are a real and serious issue for some children with developmental disorders. Ready, Set, Potty! works whether you use food as rewards or not. The important thing to remember is that your rewards have to be something your child would do anything for. Some parents who have successfully used the Ready, Set, Potty! program have provided their children with their favorite food only during the potty training process, but it is recommended that parents check with their child's doctor before using food as rewards if your child has significant food allergy issues.

Question 16: Does Ready, Set, Potty! work only for children with special needs?

Answer: No. Ready, Set, Potty! has been used as a potty training program for children with special needs, as well as neuro-typical children, with both experiencing a high degree of success.

Question 17: I have used several potty training programs with no success. In the past, whenever I tried a new potty training program, my child developed some undesirable behavior issues. Will my child develop behavior issues with Ready, Set, Potty!?

Answer: Behavior issues are not the result of potty training; they occur as your child tries to find ways to maneuver through the new information he or she is presented with, and as a way to problem solve a concept for which he or she does not possess the skills. One of the neat aspects of the Ready, Set, Potty! program is that because of its relevance and direction, coupled with the institution of order, predictability, and routine, a child promptly begins to acquire new skills in a very non-threatening manner. Remember, Ready, Set, Potty! is an individualized program that caters to your child's individual learning mode, and one that introduces concepts along with skills to help your child navigate through his or her new environment.

Question 18: What if my child is not reinforced by food, and is motivated by very few activities?

Answer: It is humanly impossible for any of us not to like anything, or anyone. In order to begin a successful potty training program, parents must evaluate—along with the child's teachers and therapist—what interests the child most, or who is of significant importance to the child. As long as we are alive, we have likes and dislikes, and needs and wants. A process of evaluation and discovery must take place in order to understand the best strategies to use in your individualized potty training program; this process is critical to potty training success.

Question 19: I have two children with special needs, which of the two do I potty train first?

Answer: Potty train the child with the most severe disability; doing so will facilitate the process for your other child. Do not attempt to potty train both of them at the same time—doing so will quickly turn your potty training program into a frustrating endeavor for you and for your children.

Question 20: Can I use a potty training video or a potty doll to help my child potty train?

Answer: Ready, Set, Potty! does not recommend the use of a potty training video, or a potty doll. A potty training video would only become entertainment for your child, and a potty training doll communicates to your child that as long as the doll has gone to the toilet, he or she does not have to go. You can use yourself and other family members as models if you must, but make sure that you reward yourself immediately after modeling the potty behavior for your child, and that you tell him or her that it is his or her turn to go to the toilet.

As you can see, there are many questions parents and teachers have, and continue to ask in regard to potty training. I hope that I have covered all the questions that I know will help you gain confidence in using Ready, Set, Potty! as your potty training program. Remember that from the minute you decide to use this program, you have already set yourself and your child up for success.

CHAPTER 13
CLOSING REMARKS

Congratulations on your decision to embark on the beginning of your child's road to independence, a road that is filled with exciting new ventures for both you and your child. We have come to the end of the Ready, Set, Potty! program, and to the beginning of your potty training success; congratulate yourself on believing and knowing that you can and will help your child achieve potty training independence. My deepest desire is that this book has helped you prepare for successfully potty training your child with special needs. My prayer for you is that as you walk through this, our journey, you gather knowledge, courage, enthusiasm, and determination to teach your child with significance, perseverance, and success. I wish for you and your child a potty training experience that is strengthened by your challenges and victories, a potty training experience that you will meet with success as your only option.

I want to thank you for making a connection with me by reading this book, and I want to congratulate you on the first step towards potty training success. Keep in touch by writing to me at postmaster@focussped.com and let me know about your potty training challenges and victories; I would love to hear from you. Take care of yourself and of your precious angel, and see you on the journey.

Until always,
Brenda Batts

INDEX